# LIGHTHOUSE
## OF WALES

*South Stack Lighthouse - William Daniell (1815),*
*(By permission of the National Library of Wales).*

On South Stack rock what glories feast our eyes,
Entrance our senses and our souls surprise!
To paint each scene no colours can be found
Romantic beauties crowd the enchanted ground.

(Thomas Jackson, R.N., *Handbook for Holyhead* (London, 1853).

*Whitford Point, West Glamorgan.*

# LIGHTHOUSES
## OF WALES

THEIR ARCHITECTURE AND ARCHAEOLOGY

## Douglas B. Hague

*Edited by*
Stephen Hughes

**Royal Commission on the Ancient and Historical Monuments of Wales**

ISBN 1-871184-08-8

Printed in Wales by
Mid Wales Litho Limited
Pontyfelin Industrial Estate, Pontypool, Gwent NP4 0DG. *Telephone* – 0495 750033 *Facsimile* – 0495 751466

## Royal Commission on the Ancient and Historical Monuments of Wales
## Crown Building, Plas Crug, Aberystwyth, Dyfed, SY23 1NJ
*Telephone* - 0970 624381    *Fax* - 0970 627701

The Commission was established in 1908 to make an inventory of the ancient and historical monuments of
Wales and Monmouthshire. It is currently empowered by a Royal Warrent of 1992 to survey, record, publish
and maintain a database of ancient and historical sites, structures and landscapes in Wales. It is also
responsible for the National Monuments Record of Wales which is open daily for public reference, for the
supply of archaeological information to the Ordance Survey for mapping purposes and the co-ordination of
archaeological aerial photography in Wales.

# Contents

*South Bishop Lighthouse,*
*Dyfed (Pembrokeshire).*

# Douglas B. Hague,    1917 ~ 1990

Douglas Hague trained as an architect and went on to be an investigator with the Royal Commission on Ancient and Historical Monuments in Wales from 1948 until 1981. He was a pioneer, with Morgan Rees, of the subject of industrial archaeology in Wales in the 1960s and '70s and he did much to create public awareness of the significance of such well-known monuments as the Conwy Suspension Bridge and the quarry workshops at Dinorwig. He also recorded fast-disappearing industrial monuments all over Wales and the results of this work are preserved in the Royal Commission's National Monuments Record for Wales. His influence extended over Britain and overseas. His interests and expertise was felt over a wide field and he was heavily involved in the activities of a host of societies and groups, including the Royal Archaeological Institute and the Victorian Society. In recognition of his contribution to the subject, he was invited to become Vice-President of the Association for Industrial Archaeology in 1987. His wide range of archaeological and architectural articles and other writings included contributions on churches to the three volumes of the Royal Commission's *Inventory of the Ancient Monuments of Caernarvonshire* (1956-64) and the section on castles in the *Glamorgan County History, the Middle Ages* (1971). Douglas Hague's work was crowned with the publication in 1975 of *Lighthouses*, a seminal work of international interest, written jointly with Rosemary Christie, on the archaeology and history of a group of monuments for which he had a particular fascination. One of his great loves was the study of the islands of the Welsh coast, and he contributed to the Royal Commission's files a considerable body of material on their lighthouses as well as on many aspects of their archaeology. He drew on this material in his study on *The Lighthouses of Wales* which he published in the *The Archaeological Journal* in 1979. He died in September 1990 without being able to publish a further projected work on the subject in book form. This has now been undertaken by his colleague, Stephen Hughes, who worked with Douglas Hague from 1973 to 1981 on the industrial archaeology of Wales. He has now compiled the present *Lighthouses of Wales* largely from the latter's notes and articles on the subject, together with his informative and attractive scale-drawings and photographs.

Lighthouses in Wales* is an important addition to the Royal Commission's publications on industrial archaeology which already include *A guide and study in Waterways Archaeology: The Archaeology of the Montgomeryshire Canal* and *The Archaeology of an Early Railway System: The Brecon Forest Tramroads*; and, published jointly with other bodies, *The Industrial Archaeology of the Swansea Region* and *Frongoch Lead and Zinc Mine. Lighthouses of Wales* and *Early Railways of Wales* are the first in a new series which will provide the locations and other details of important categories of monuments over the whole of Wales.

**Beverley Smith** (*Chairman*).

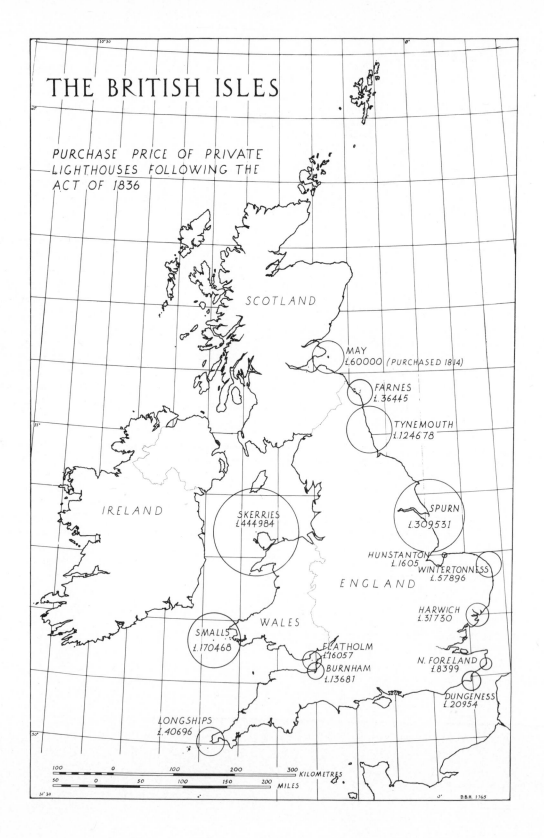

# THE BRITISH ISLES

PURCHASE PRICE OF PRIVATE
LIGHTHOUSES FOLLOWING THE
ACT OF 1836

SCOTLAND

MAY
£60000 (PURCHASED 1814)

FARNES
£36445

TYNEMOUTH
£124678

IRELAND

SKERRIES
£444984

SPURN
£309531

HUNSTANTON
£1605

WINTERTONNESS
£57896

ENGLAND

HARWICH
£31730

WALES

SMALLS
£170468

FLATHOLM
£16057

BURNHAM
£13681

N. FORELAND
£8399

DUNGENESS
£20954

LONGSHIPS
£40696

| 100 | 0 | 100 | 200 | 300 |
|-----|---|-----|-----|-----|

KILOMETRES

| 50 | 0 | 50 | 100 | 150 | 200 |

MILES

D.B.H. 1965

# Introduction

Despite Britain's decline as a maritime power, the coasts of Wales, England and Scotland are still better lit than those of most other countries. Although many of our lighthouses are now unmanned, the buildings remain as testimony to the courage, enterprise and invention of their builders.

The lighthouses of Wales form an interesting and compact group, administered by Trinity House with the exception of minor harbour lights. They are closely bound to each other by ties of economic history. Major navigation routes of world importance lay along the coasts of Wales and the ample dues claimed from this dense shipping activity financed the large number of lighthouses around the north and south shores and their adjoining headlands, together with the associated lights of the English shores of Liverpool Bay and the Severn Estuary. These economic ties involve practices which are not generally known and are worth a short explanation.

## Economic history

The earliest charter granted to Trinity House is dated 1514, but it was not until 1566, with the issue of a confirmation of the charter, that we find the first mention of the powers of the Brotherhood to erect lighthouses. Its most important functions had been pilotage on the River Thames and charitable work among aged seamen and their dependants. In such circumstances they would, if they could, avoid the risks and uncertainties of building lighthouses by adopting the practice, common amongst quasi-official bodies before the days of the established Civil Service, of contracting out ('farming') to private individuals. This practice did work, although it is natural to think that any person prepared to take such a risk would have harboured motives which were not wholly altruistic. There were cases of naive and philanthropic builders who lost their money, and who were persuaded to follow the example of their more astute colleagues and acquire a patent or authority from the Crown to collect dues from ships passing the lights. This was usually done

*Huge revenues were available from lighthouses on prime routes. The owners of the Smalls and Skerries sold their interests to Trinity House for vast sums.*

by a collector, or a customs officer acting on his behalf when a ship made a British port. At times this collection of dues became not only retrospective but anticipatory (in expectation) of the vessel's return voyage, and the behaviour of some collectors, particularly towards the masters of foreign ships, was to cause considerable international friction.

With the vast increase in the volume of western trade the revenues of the proprietors of the private lighthouse grew, in some cases prodigiously. What had been altruistic speculations became jealously held privileges. So excessive were the profits and so avaricious the operators that this eventually precipitated the Act of 1836 under which Trinity House was empowered to buy out all privately owned lighthouses. In Scotland, the Northern Lighthouse Board purchased the May lighthouse, but in Ireland the anomaly of privately owned lighthouses had been eliminated in the early eighteenth century.

The Welsh lighthouses at the Smalls and on the Skerries were pre-eminent examples of the means by which huge incomes were generated from passing shipping. The most tenacious, or even avaricious, owners in Britain were the proprietors of the lights on the Skerries and, in England, of the Spurn and Tynemouth lighthouses. These operators, or their ancestors, had been lucky or cunning enough to have had their leases granted in perpetuity. Whereas it was possible to work out a fair amount of compensation for a lease which had a definite number of years to run, the term *'in perpetuity'* presents a problem for the most able actuary.

The proprietors of the two English lights, at Spurn Head and Tynemouth, were richly rewarded to the extent of £124,678 and £309,531, but the executors of Morgan Jones II of the Skerries led the field of those compensated for the loss of receipts *'in perpetuity'* with £444,984 (that is some £25,825,000 at 1988 monetary values). This sum, which was awarded by a Beaumaris jury, is a monument to the dogged perseverance of Morgan Jones's Cardigan solicitor and is an indictment of the system which made this sort of thing possible and legal. As can be imagined, Trinity House had difficulty in laying hands on funds to pay this vast compensation, but they managed to do so and, what is more, made a special effort to improve the stations involved, as can so clearly be seen at the Skerries.

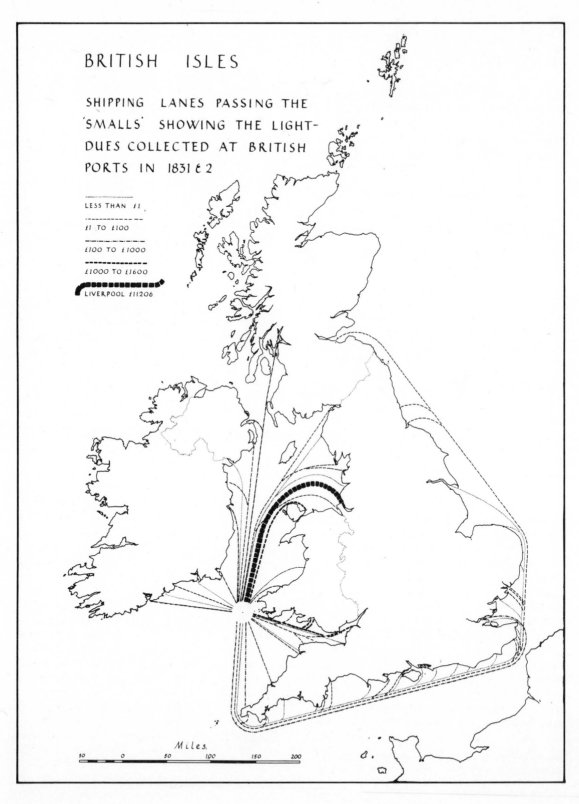

BRITISH ISLES

SHIPPING LANES PASSING THE
'SMALLS' SHOWING THE LIGHT-
DUES COLLECTED AT BRITISH
PORTS IN 1831 & 2

LESS THAN £1
£1 TO £100
£100 TO £1000
£1000 TO £1600
LIVERPOOL £11206

Miles.

50    0    50    100    150    200

# The historical distribution of lighthouses

The earliest British lights tended to be situated on the south and south-east coasts of England in order to assist continental traffic, including the great wine trade from France; later, by the seventeenth century, the emphasis changed a little with lights to the east to help colliers carrying coal from the north-east down to London. Later, with the opening of colonial trade with the west in the eighteenth and nineteenth centuries, London still remained the largest port but the overall balance changed to the west coast of Britain and was eventually dominated by Liverpool. The Liverpool Harbour Authority was set up in 1762 and the emergence of Liverpool as the major port of western Britain is illustrated by the statistics. Between the years 1772 and 1805, inward shipping, largely from America and the West Indies, including such cargoes as tobacco and sugar, increased from 77,000 to 331,000 tons. Salt exports between 1790 and 1820 increased tenfold and coal exports were notable. However an ignominious stigmatic record was achieved when Liverpool's slave-trade eclipsed that of London and Bristol. It was because of this change in the pattern of trade that the need to light the Welsh coast arose.

The dominance of the Liverpool trade alongside the Welsh coast is illustrated by the evidence of the lighthouse dues collected from ships passing the Smalls Lighthouse in Pembrokeshire in 1831-32. £11,206 (£650,396 at 1988 monetary values) was collected from ships docking in Liverpool, while trade to Swansea, Neath, Bristol and Beaumaris was only worth between £1,000 and £1,600 in dues for each port. Trade from Belfast, Dublin, Wexford, Cork, Glasgow, London and Hayle (Cornwall) was worth between £100 and £1,000 in dues paid and another 52 British ports contributing paid less than £100 in dues each.

The early dominance by Bristol of trade westwards along the south Wales coast, evidenced in the very name of the Bristol Channel, was later challenged by the great coal ports of south Wales and eventually by the magnificent natural harbour of Milford Haven. These changes are reflected in the evolving pattern of lighthouse construction.

*The interest of Liverpool in building the Smalls Lighthouse is explained by the structure's crucial importance in lighting the sea-lane leading southwards from that port.*

*The pre-eminence of the sea-lane alongside west Wales is clearly shown by this map.*

By the mid-nineteenth century the western trade routes of Britain had become clearly dominant in British trade, and consequently the dues paid to the owners of the Skerries Lighthouse (off Anglesey) and the Smalls Lighthouse (off Pembrokeshire) were greater by far than those paid to any other lighthouse in the British Isles. Some £23,000 was paid for the use of the Smalls light in 1852, about £18,000 for the Skerries, then followed the dues paid to three lights off Land's End, the Mersey and East Anglia which yielded lesser figures of between £9,000 and £13,000. Other lighthouses in the British Isles tended to raise £5,000 or below in annual revenue. (By 1822 the standard lighthouse due collected at British ports was one farthing per ton.)

# Lighthouse types

Lighthouses fall neatly into two classes, those built on rocks in the sea and those on the land; although their purposes may be the same, they differ or overlap. At the top of the first class is the *'conventional'* lighthouse, a lonely tower breaking the horizon and rising directly from the sea which belabours it relentlessly. No other building is subject to such furious and outrageous batterings and all fittings have to match those used at sea. Consequently their design and construction are of incomparable quality; bereft of decoration, they display that rare kind of chaste beauty, the expression of pure functionalism. Some towers on tall rocks or islets may be set out of reach of the sea, but their building involved the same superhuman difficulties of access.

No one will ever know the site of the first navigational light displayed in Wales. A Roman date has been suggested at various times for possible lighthouse towers at Flint and Holyhead. However, a reasonable case can be made for a medieval lighthouse at St Ann's Head. Chronologically later is Flatholm in the Bristol Channel, followed by the Skerries off the north-west tip of Anglesey, but here lighthouses will be described geographically, from north-east to south-east.

To those whose experience of landing on an island is limited to driving a car off a ferry, the immense difficulties of making a landing on an exposed rock cannot be imagined. To sail and then to row a fragile boat carrying dressed stones weighing over a ton into the proximity of the very hazards of which the lighthouse was to be a warning demands a degree of skill, bravery and patience seldom surpassed in any human endeavour. Even today with all the advantages of powered craft, pneumatic drills, mobile tools and helicopters, we should respect the achievements of lighthouse builders.

It has generally been considered, certainly by British authors, that the first rock-lighthouse was the Eddystone Lighthouse (22.5km or 14 miles south-south-west of Plymouth) of 1698, but over 500 years earlier, by 1157, the Pisans had built a tower on Meloria Reef some 6.5km or 4 miles off Livorno. This was destroyed by the Genoese in 1284 (the site is now occupied by an interesting arched structure built in 1712), but from the replacement tower which the Pisans built in more sheltered waters in 1302, and which survived until destroyed by the Germans in the last war, the design of the original structure can be reasonably deduced. It had a battered lower storey or solid base supporting two cylindrical drums with a decrease in diameter about half-way up. However the oldest surviving rock

tower was not conceived in this way. This is the magnificent French lighthouse of Cordouan in the Gironde. Started in 1584, this 'self-indulgent' structure contained a royal chapel and king's hall and was more richly ornamented than any tower before or since. Almost before the last obelisk and acroterion had been fixed in position the island became eroded, but fortunately there was time to protect the tower by a massive encircling wall containing store-rooms which still survive. This makes Cordouan the oldest rock tower by accident. Its exuberant external decoration was removed when extensive rebuilding and heightening took place in the late eighteenth century.

The first half of the nineteenth century saw the erection of most of the great rock towers off the coasts of Britain, whilst in the second half of the century the great increase in shipping, particularly of regular steamship sailings, necessitated the building of many smaller harbour lights. In Wales the only true wave-washed rock tower is the Smalls, off the Pembrokeshire coast, but other notable rock towers are the nearby South Bishop and the Skerries, both set on rocky islets.

Less need be said of the second class of lighthouse, those built on land. Although some lights erected on piers can be subjected to conditions almost equal to those on exposed rock sites, most do not present anything like the same difficulties of building. A major factor affecting their appearance is their function and site: clearly a warning light situated on top of a high cliff calls for little more than a lantern on a squat tower, whereas if situated on lower-lying ground a tall tower may be required.

# Materials of tower construction

The traditional material for building lighthouses is stone, particularly in such buildings as the Smalls where specially designed and keyed blocks were used. Good stone was usually imported. In order to build the Smalls Lighthouse over 3,000 tons of Cornish granite were quarried from the de Lank workings near Bodmin and shipped to Trinity Quay at Solva where it was worked and fitted to the designs for the new lighthouse.[1] A new steam-tug, *'Solva'*, was specially built to tow two 40 ton barges

*The Skerries Lighthouse is one of the notable rock-towers off the Welsh coast. The crow-stepped gables top the keeper's detached house.*

**An Estimate made by Mr. Hamilton and Mr. Meredith of the Expense of erecting a Lighthouse upon the same Construction as the Hoylake one, which is 52 foot high. Diameter at the Bottom from out to out 25ft. 9 in. Do. at the Top 16 foot.**[2]

| | £ | s | d |
|---|---|---|---|
| Height of the 2 Brick and half work 23 foot; Diameter 24 foot. Contents 189 yards (The Morter for the outside to the half Lime and the middle of the wall flushed & supposing Brick can be made near the Spot) at 6s per yard | 56 | 14 | 0 |
| Height of two Brick work 29 foot, Diameter 20 foot, 4 Inches Contents 192 yards at 4s 9¾d per | 46 | 3 | 11 |
| Brick work round the Stairs height 37 foot, Circumference 24 foot—Contents 98 yards 6 foot at 2s 3d | 11 | 0 | 6 |
| Two Chimneys 40 yards, brick breadth, but char'd double on account of the Wings, Arches & Plastering at 2s 3d per yd | 4 | 10 | 0 |
| Brick floor at the Bottom 42yds at 1s | 2 | 2 | 0 |
| Twelve square yds brick length for a Coalhouse in the Inside at 2s 3d | 1 | 7 | 0 |
| Brick work about the Lamp | 0 | 12 | 0 |
| Eight Door Cases & Linteles all Deal at 12s per Seven Window Frames, Oak, 3 foot square, Linteles & Boards, at the bottoms & Slides at 10s per | 3 | 10 | 0 |
| 7 windows, glaz'd with Common Glass & Journey to put them in | 2 | 18 | 0 |
| Sash frame of Oak for the Light 9 foot long & 8 foot high | 3 | 0 | 0 |
| Glazing Do. & Journey | 4 | 10 | 0 |
| 57 Steps of Ash 7½ Inch rise including Bearers, newel posts and making good the vacancies at 4s per | 11 | 8 | 0 |
| A Lead Sink in the Kitchen, frame, pipe thro' the Wall | 2 | 10 | 0 |
| Locks, Hinges, Latches and Catches | 1 | 0 | 0 |
| Bulk Head to close in the Stairs at the Top | 2 | 18 | 0 |
| Two partitions in the Rooms with Doors | 3 | 0 | 0 |
| Six Deal summers for 3 Floors 156 foot at 1s 2d | 9 | 2 | 0 |
| Three hundred & 81 foot of Deal Joyce for Do. at 2½d | 3 | 16 | 0 |
| Laying down the Beams & Joyces | 1 | 10 | 0 |
| Eight hundred 55 foot of flooring Boards for do. at 3d | 10 | 13 | 0 |
| Laying the same & Nails | 2 | 10 | 0 |
| Twenty six yards of Flagging in the Light room & finding Plaister to bed the same in at 3/6 | 4 | 11 | 0 |
| Plaistering & rendering the Light Room | 3 | 10 | 0 |
| Sixty four foot of Oak summer running measure for the Roof at 1/6 per | 4 | 16 | 0 |
| Eighty foot of Spar for Do. at 2½ & Corb for do. 5/- | 1 | 1 | 8 |
| One hundred & 92 foot of Oak Board for Do. to carry the Load on the Roof at 3d per foot | 2 | 8 | 0 |
| Workmanship in the Roof & Nails | 1 | 10 | 0 |
| Twenty hundred of Lead for Roof at 25s per | 25 | 0 | 0 |
| Solder for Do | 4 | 10 | 0 |
| Lead Cistern for the Oil 3 foot square, solder & Workmanship | 6 | 6 | 0 |
| Wood Frame for Do | 0 | 10 | 0 |
| Lead Cistern for Water in the Light room & pipe to convey it from the roof thro' the Walls, solder & Workmanship | 5 | 5 | 0 |
| Six Stones for Balcony 4 foot by 26 foot & 5 Inch thick very hard, come from Up: Holland working & setting the same | 7 | 16 | 0 |
| Iron Work for Balcony to be railed double | 5 | 14 | 0 |
| Coping Stone round the Top | 3 | 0 | 0 |
| Painting | 3 | 0 | 0 |
| Slabbing under the foundation with Oak plank 2 inch thick or a Stone foundation will be much the same price | 5 | 0 | 0 |
| Copper for the Oil to feed the Lamp | 1 | 0 | 0 |
| Building a Wash house, Cow house and Necessary house larger than the Hoylake one, with a Loft for Hay etc | 50 | 0 | 0 |
| Boatage of Timber, Lime, Lead & Flagg etc suppos'd to be | 25 | 0 | 0 |
| B. If Brick is to be carried it will be £25 more— | | | |
| | 349 | 8 | 1 |

*Note—There are 4 Floors in the Hoylake Lighthouse as two families live therein as they are oblig'd to take care of two Lighthouses—but the Calculation for the Air Light is only made for 3 floors the same being sufficient—If a Lighthouse be built not more than 25 foot high & lighted with a Coal fire W. Hamilton judges, it will be less expence in building by £150 and the Construction sho'd be somewhat different.*

out to the Smalls loaded with the worked stones and other necessary building materials. One hundred construction workers were based at Solva while the masonry tower on the Smalls rock was being completed in 1858-61. Elsewhere local stone was used for infillings or secondary building (a contemporary painting of South Stack shows this being done). The surviving intact stone-built structure of the formerly coal-fired lighthouse at Mumbles, Swansea, is the most complete example of its type left in Britain.

Bridgewater brick was shipped to the South Bishop, and Point of Ayr was also constructed of brick, as the surviving builders estimate (a rare survival) of 1776 shows (*see opposite*).

The original and unique Smalls Lighthouse, as completed, was significant for its being the first lighthouse ever built with an upper structure supported on stanchions, posts or piles. At first, in 1775, this was of composite construction with three piles of cast-iron and a number of timber secured in post-holes dug into the surface of the Smalls Rock. The upper part of the timbers flexed in gales but the iron did not and the structure was in danger of tearing itself apart. In 1776 it was rebuilt as a completely timber structure and lasted successfully until 1812 when it started breaking up after a working life of 36 years.

The attempt to use the new constructional material of cast-iron was unprecedented as conceived in 1773-74. This pre-dates the famous Ironbridge in Shropshire, and may be the first time constructional cast-iron members were used in the world after their earlier use for window lintels and simple bridges in the China of the first millennium. In south Wales the proximity of the ironworks and foundries led to the construction of a number of lights made completely of cast-iron. The west pier of the great new copper-importing port of Swansea was crowned with a cast-iron tower in 1802 but the most interesting existing example in Wales is at Whitford Point, Glamorgan. The use of copper roof-sheeting on the demolished works of 'Copperopolis' is also reflected in the unique surviving copper sheets and glazing-bars of the Whitford Point Lighthouse.

In north Wales another piled light was built, this time almost completely of iron. This light constructed at Point of Ayr in 1843-44 was one of a new generation of piled lights built in the British Isles in the 1840s and 1850s - Wyre, near Fleetwood (1840); Maplin (1841); Gunfleet (1850); Mucking (1851) and Spit Bank, Cork (1853). Several of these used

Alexander Mitchell's cast-iron screwpile (patented in the 1830s) in order to drive in their foundations, and Mitchell was contracted to fix the piles on these lighthouses with James Walker designing the superstructures. Both Point of Ayr and Mucking were not screwed-pile structures but instead cylinders sunk into sand formed their foundations. At Point of Ayr workmen sunk 1.4m (4ft 6in) diameter wrought-iron cylinders into the sand exposed at low water. Within each of these a smaller 1.14m (3ft 9in) diameter cast-iron cylinder was sunk by the expedient of digging sand from the inside until each 2.7m (9ft) long cylinder was sunk 3.7m (12ft) into the sand. Within these again were lowered 3.96m (13ft) long hollow cast-iron pillars which were then set in concrete topped by 0.3m (1ft) thick stones. There were eight such inclined struts centred on a vertical central pillar with a combined weight of 90 tons.[3] The iron superstructure of the lighthouse sat on these legs. This light lasted almost forty years until replaced by a small lightship in December 1883. Other contemporary lights, such as Spit Bank at Cork and the much rebuilt Wyre Lighthouse, have survived.

In its turn concrete has replaced iron as a wondrous new material and in recent times reinforced concrete has been used to construct lights (functioning as guidance or 'leading' beacons) at the oil-importing harbour at Milford Haven.

# The engineers

Specialist lighthouse engineers, such as Joseph Nelson or James Walker, are not generally as well known as, for example, their contemporaries who worked on canals or railways; but, .in somewhat more obscure locations, they did equally valuable work in completing the necessary infrastructure for the efficient bulk carriage of the goods of the world's first industrial revolution. Others involved included the famous civil engineers John Rennie and Jesse Hartley and the Welsh-based architects H. Turner and William Jernegan.

Henry Whiteside was a long-serving engineer/agent for the Smalls lighthouse, rather different from his itinerant and more prolific colleagues. By

[1] E. Freeman, *The Solva Saga* (Llanblethian, 1958), 10-11.

[2] City of Chester Record Office, CB 165.

[3] G. I. Hawkes, 'The Point of Ayr Lighthouses', Cymru a'r Môr: Maritime Wales **9** (1985), 32-43.

1775 he had established himself at the *'Old Ship Inn'*, near the shore base for the construction of the lighthouse at Solva, and later married the proprietor's daughter. He decided to experience the conditions of the new Smalls Light on 13 January 1777, and was promptly marooned there with the crew by the adverse weather conditions. The light was extinguished by the gales and distress messages were sent in bottles encased in wooden casks (the lighthouse engineers obviously experienced conditions as hazardous as the keepers). His letter, addressed to Thomas Williams, magistrate, proprietor of one of the local silver mines and the Trinity House Representative in Solva, ran as follows:

*To* Mr. Williams. Smalls.

February 1, 1777.

Sir,

Being now in a most dangerous and distressed condition upon the Smalls, do hereby trust Providence will bring to your hand this, which prayeth for your immediate assistance to fetch us off the Smalls before the next spring or we fear we shall all perish; our water near all gone, our fire quite gone, and our house in a most melancholy manner. I doubt not but you will fetch us from here as fast as possible; we can be got off at some part of the tide almost any weather. I need say no more, but remain your distressed,

Humble Servant,

Hy. Whiteside.

We were distressed in a gale of wind upon the 13th of January, since which have not been able to keep any light; but we could not have kept any light above sixteen nights longer for want of oil and candles, which makes us murmur and think we are forgotten,

Ed. Edwardes,

Geo. Adams,

Jno. Price.

We doubt not but that whoever takes up this will be so merciful as to cause it to be sent to Thos. Williams, Esq., Trelethin, near St. David's, Wales.[4]

One of the three casks arrived in Solva Harbour three days later and Whiteside and the crew were relieved. Phillips, the lessee of the Smalls Rock, had died by this stage and the enterprising Whiteside was given perpetual management of the lighthouse and a house which was built at Gamlyn, overlooking the *'New Quay'*. This dwelling, called *'Harbour House'*, still remains at Solva. Whiteside was still in charge in 1812 when he had to answer more cask-borne messages from distressed lighthouse-keepers.

*Some details of the better-known engineers are given in the following section:*

# Daniel Asher Alexander (1768-1846)

Alexander succeeded Samuel Wyatt as Consultant Engineer to Trinity House in 1807. His first lighthouse was the South Stack (Holyhead) of 1809. This was followed, outside Wales, by the Inner Farne and Heligoland Lighthouses of 1811 and the Hurst Lighthouse of 1812. The nine-sided brick lighthouse at Harwich, and accompanying low light were built between 1818 and 1822, and these, with the circular granite-built Lundy (Old) Lighthouse (on an island off the south Wales coast), had cavity walls.

Sources: *Dictionary of National Biography* and H.M. Colvin, *A Biographical Dictionary of British Architects 1660-1840* (1978).

# Sir James Nicholas Douglass (1826-98)

Engineer-in-chief to Trinity House, 1863-92. He had assisted his father, Nicholas, in building the ill-fated iron tower on the Bishop Rock, designed by James Walker in 1847, and built the stone tower which replaced it. He was resident engineer on the Smalls from 1855 to its completion in 1861 when he was transferred to the Wolf Rock. After his appointment as Engineer-in-chief he designed twenty new towers, including the new Eddystone and the reconstructed Bishop Rock. In 1864 he invented the helically framed lantern.

Sources: T. Williams, *Life of Sir James N. Douglass* (1900); *Dictionary of National Biography* and obituary in *Minutes of the Proceedings of the Institution of Civil Engineers*.

# Jesse Hartley (1780-1860)

Hartley was born in Pontefract into a family of masons and architects. He was engineer for the Bolton and Manchester Railway and Canal, and Chief Engineer to the Mersey Docks and Harbour Board until 1860. In this latter capacity he designed the lighthouses at Point Lynas, Anglesey (1835), and at Crosby, Lancashire (1847).

Sources: Q. Hughes, *Seaport* (1964); *Dictionary of*

---

[4]E. Freeman, *The Solva Saga* (Llanblethian. 1958), 5-9.

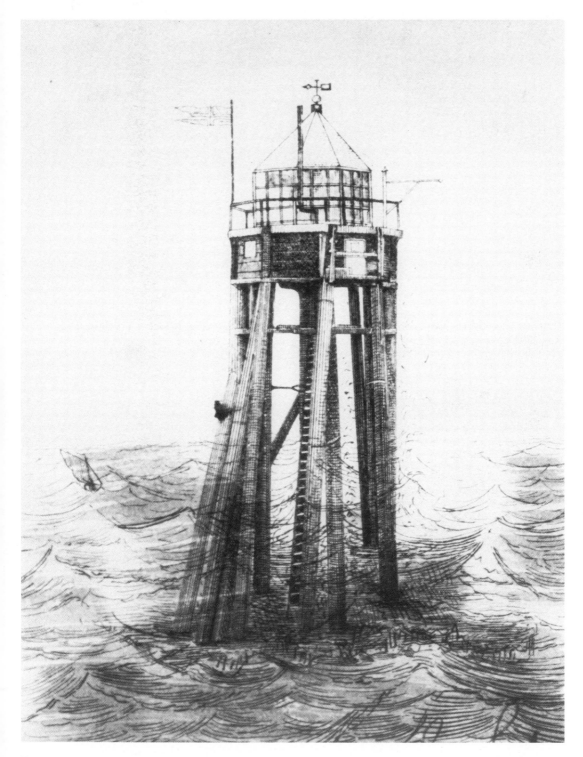

*Henry Whiteside's pioneering pile-built light on the Smalls Rock*     *(By permission of the National Library of Wales).*

*National Biography*; Colvin, *Dictionary of British Architects*, entry for Bernard Hartley.

## William Jernegan (1750-1836)

A well-known Swansea architect, who worked in the classical style, but also produced designs for one of the Swansea copper-smelting works in 1790, for the stone-built octagonal Mumbles Lighthouse in 1793, and the now destroyed cast-iron lighthouse on Swansea west pier in 1803.

Sources: W. Jernegan, Design-drawings for a copper-works (1790), in the National Library of Wales; W.H. Jones, *History of the Port of Swansea* (Carmarthen, 1922); Colvin, *Dictionary of British Architects*.

## George F. Lyster

Lyster succeeded John B. Hartley as Engineer-in-chief to the Mersey Docks and Harbour Board. He designed and constructed Great Orme's Head Lighthouse in 1862 and altered Point Lynas in 1871.

Source: *Liverpool Daily Post*, Commemorative Issue, 1927.

## Sir Thomas Matthews (1849-1930)

Matthews was Engineer-in-chief to Trinity House 1892-1915. He designed Spurn Head in 1895, Pendeen in 1900, and Skokholm in 1915.

## Joseph Nelson ( -1833)

Nelson was a native of Whitkirk, Leeds, where he died. His name is associated with at least fifteen lighthouses, and he is first recorded as builder of the South Stack near Holyhead, designed by Daniel Alexander in 1809. He was then engaged to build the two English lights on the Inner Farne in 1809-10. In 1826 he returned to the area as engineer of the Longstone Lighthouse. He built several Welsh lighthouses including the square tower on Bardsey in 1821 and others on each side of the Bristol Channel, notably the Nash Lighthouses in Glamorgan. His Berwick pier light of 1826 shows the influence of Daniel Alexander's Harwich Lighthouse.

Source: D.B. Hague, *Country Life*, 11 February 1965.

## John Rennie (1761-1821)

Rennie, born at Phantassie farm in East Lothian, was one of the most eminent civil engineers of the Industrial Revolution. His role in the design of the Bell Rock Lighthouse has been clouded in acrimonious debate for one hundred and fifty years. Robert Stevenson, the resident engineer, later insisted that he alone was responsible for the design, but this was challenged by Rennie's son, Sir John, in his autobiography, and strongly disputed by the Stevenson family since. Whilst engaged on the harbour installations for the Irish Mail Packet Service, Rennie designed lighthouses at Howth and Holyhead.

Sources: J. Rennie, *The Autobiography of Sir John Rennie* (1875); C.T.G. Boucher, *John Rennie 1761-1821. The life and work of a great engineer* (Manchester, 1963); *Dictionary of National Biography*; Colvin, *Dictionary of British Architects*.

## James Walker (1781-1862)

Walker was born in Glasgow but became an engineer articled to his uncle Ralph Walker in London. Here he became involved with the increased building of docks. Although continuing to practise with his partners, Burges and Cooper, he was appointed consultant engineer to Trinity House for whom he (or sometimes his firm) designed some 29 towers, the earliest being at west Usk, Newport, in 1821. Where there was room, as on the Pembrokeshire and Anglesey lighthouses of the South Bishop and Skerries, he produced stylish layouts for ancillary buildings with attractive sheltered courtyards. He also paid attention to sanitation, and the Smalls (Pembrokeshire) and Wolf Lighthouse (Cornwall) rock towers were the first to be planned with proper water-closets. His designs for rock towers greatly improved after the rather unsatisfactory Bishop Rock. The Needles (Isle of Wight) of 1859 had perpendicular sides, whilst the exposed Smalls (1861) and Wolf Rock (1870) illustrate his use of the stepped base which broke the waves and discouraged seas from sweeping up the tower, as was the case at Eddystone and Bell Rock.

Source: Obituary in the *Minutes of the Institution of Civil Engineers*.

## Henry Whiteside (1748-1824)

Whiteside remains one of the most mysterious and enigmatic characters ever to be connected with lighthouse construction. Whiteside was a musical-instrument maker and, in our present state of knowledge, it is very difficult to understand why

*The lantern and optic of George Lyster's Great Orme Lighthouse*    (NMR: Howarth-Loomes Collection).

John Phillips, the Liverpool Dock-master, should have instructed him to make a model for a proposed new lighthouse on the Skerries, off Anglesey, in 1772, and in the following year to prepare one for a light on the Smalls, off the coast of Pembrokeshire. Nothing is known of his model or of his design for the Skerries, but his ingenious design for the Smalls was accepted and work commenced in 1774.

Whiteside supervised the work himself and on its completion stayed in the light to observe its behaviour. All that is likely to be known of Whiteside and his achievement is to be found in an article on the Smalls by E.C. Woods and J. Rees in the *Transactions of the Lancashire and Cheshire Historical Society* (1948). *See* also E. Freeman, *The Solva Saga* (1958).

19

*Originally unlit marker on Llanddwyn Island, Anglesey, now with a modern light added.*

# Methods of illumination

Here we deal with the central reason for the need to provide any of these large lighthouse structures. The type of fuel used had a fundamental effect on the design and appearance of lighthouses. However, these lit guides for mariners had been themselves preceded by unlit markers.

## Unlit beacons, day- or sea-marks

A maritime beacon is a sign, or navigation mark, which is usually unlit. Most are set on headlands and a distinctive unnatural silhouette is required to stand out in marked contrast to any growing or geographical feature.

The origins of many such structures are very obscure, but a Roman date has been claimed for at least one coastal feature.[5] The so called 'Roman Pharos at Flint' stood at an altitude of 247m (809ft) on Coed-y-garreg, the highest point of the parish of Whitford Garn, a short distance to the west of the parish church. The 'Pharos' was shown on Williamson's Chart of 1766. Thomas Pennant described the remains in 1796 when he assumed that it had been a lighthouse to guide mariners approaching Roman Chester. The structure was circular with an inner diameter of 3.8m (12.5ft) and had walls 1.32m (4ft 4in) thick with a staircase reported as leading to two floors. The tower was no longer thought worthy of note on Denham's Chart of 1837.

The modest little 'sentry-box' marker on Llanddwyn Island, Anglesey, has a 3.95m diameter structure tapering to a domed roof about 7m high (now crowned with a modern light). Less rude is the diminutive beacon at Amlwch, Anglesey. Also in Anglesey are the two Coal Rock beacons on Carmel Head. These are T-shaped in plan, presenting triangular elevations 10.35m high and some 5.5m wide. Each of the three arms of the 'T' slope back towards the central 'spire' at about 5°; they date from around 1830. Some wave-washed beacons served a dual purpose as daymarks as well as refuges for wrecked mariners.

On Ynys Dulas, in Dulas Bay (Anglesey), is a smaller tower built in 1824 by Colonel Hughes, a local landlord. He was philanthropic, but perhaps rather naive, and is said to have kept the tower stocked with flint, wood and suitable food, until he accepted the moral weakness of the local fishermen who had visited the tower regularly and depleted the

*Fig. 1. A Lighthouse on an Island or Headland, to direct Ships in the Night*
*A. the Grate  B. the Lightman stirring the Fire .*
*C. a Crane to land the Coals .*

*Fig. 2. A Porcupine to clear old Bars .*

*Lighthouse with an open fire-basket as proposed by Lewis Morris for Grassholm Island in 1748*
*(By permission of the National Library of Wales).*

stocks. It is a small circular building with a conical stone roof and a single chamber reached by steps.

The enigmatic beacon-towers on the north Wales coast must be mentioned here but, although their original purpose is not entirely clear, not one is likely to have been a lighthouse, and most are too remote from the sea to be visible to the mariner.[6]

---

[5]G.I. Hawkes, 'The Point of Ayr Lighthouses', *Cymru a'r Mor: Maritime Wales* **9** (1985), 32-43.

[6]G. Lloyd, 'Beacon Watch Towers on the North Wales Coast', *Archaeologia Cambrensis*, **113** (1964), 150-58; 'Seventeenth Century Beacons in North Wales', *Archaeologia Cambrensis*, **116** (1967), 195-97.

# Open fires

When a fire was kindled on top of a tower, common sense demanded that sufficient space should be provided to enable free circulation around the fire, and for the storage of some fuel as well as the handling and disposal of ashes. This type of tower is illustrated by extant sites outside Wales, such as Little Cumbrae, which greatly resembles the tower illustrated by Lewis Morris in 1748 as a proposal for Grassholm, off the Pembrokeshire coast. The design arrangements necessary for the hoist, or crane, to lift the fuel can still clearly be seen at the Mumbles Lighthouse at Swansea; this was the last of the British coal-fired lights to be built (1793) and is the best preserved.

It is difficult for us to appreciate or imagine the efficacy of a properly attended coal-fire. Obviously the keepers must have attained an expertise equal to that of the skilled and vanishing craft of boiler-stoking, and there is evidence that mariners preferred open-fires to either ineffective enclosed fires or to feeble oil lamps. One of the greatest difficulties in maintaining a regular fire was wind and rain. In tempestuous conditions the keepers did not care to be exposed and were apt to let the fire burn low and then throw on a large quantity of coal which had the effect of darkening the fire. (An enclosed lantern could not be kept clean, particularly on the inside, as water was not easily available.) An additional disadvantage was that columns of smoke were sometimes produced and confused with limekilns and ships were wrecked as a result. The last British coal-fired light was replaced in 1823; in Norway one coal-fired lighthouse continued in use until 1858.

# Candle lights

These were used from medieval times onwards. The obvious disadvantage of a candle when used with a reflector was that the resultant light moved away from the focal point as it burnt down. However, the makers of carriage lamps had evolved an ingenious solution to this problem whereby the candle was placed in a spring loaded cylindrical container with a restricted top; it is not known if this device was ever used in lighthouses. Candles were used in harbour lights until comparatively recent times, examples were recorded in use at Saundersfoot (Pembrokeshire), and Bridport (Somerset), as late as 1861.

# Oil-fired lights

Before the discovery of paraffin or kerosene a wide variety of oils were used. Sperm-whale oil was in general use in the British Isles until 1845, and Trinity House used a considerable amount of an animal oil known as *'pale southern oil'*. The cheaper rape-seed oil (colza), which had already been used in French lights for a number of years, then came into favour, though it was considered that sperm oil gave the better light. However, seal oil and even herring oil were used when available at attractive prices. The Port of Liverpool preferred *'best refined olive oil'*.

Most of these oils were thick, and in cold weather were reluctant to flow or respond to the capillary attraction of the wick. In order to improve the viscosity of the oil a fireplace was sometimes provided in the lantern room. At times this led to scenes of greasy domestic squalor as keepers did their cooking there. Pumps were needed to assist the upward passage of these heavy early oils to the lantern. Edward Price, keeper of the Point of Ayr Lighthouse from 1776, is recorded as being one of those who suffered problems with non-flowing oil in cold weather. The cost of oil made the lighthouse trustees ask that he experiment with large candles instead. This attempt to revert to earlier practice failed but local trustees struggled to keep the high cost of oil used to a minimum. In 1780 the keeper at the Point of Ayr Light was summoned to Chester with a sample of the cotton wick used at the lighthouse so that the Committee 'could take an account of the number of threads so as to reduce same, if it can be done properly, there being at present more oil used than the fund will maintain'.[7]

By far the most important improvement to the oil lamp was the invention in 1784 of the hollow wick by a Swiss engineer, Aimé Argand. By means of a hollow cylindrical wick and a glass chimney, air was drawn up in the middle which resulted in a cleaner and much brighter flame with the wick quickly burning on both the exposed inner and outer tubular surfaces and so producing less smoke. This invention made possible the impressive multi-wick mechanical burners of the second half of the nineteenth century which might have as many as eight concentric wicks. Another vital improvement was the rack-and-pinion wick-raiser; raising the wick

---

[7]G.I. Hawkes, 'The Point of Ayr Lighthouses', *Cymru a'r Mor: Maritime Wales* **9** (1985), 32-43.

had previously been a messy operation carried out with tweezers, and was impossible with a complicated burner.

After the highly successful oil strike of 1859 in Pennsylvania, the distribution of paraffin spread with astonishing speed. Not only was it cheaper than the existing oils but it was more volatile. This was a great advantage and meant that for most lamps the oil could simply be drawn up from the reservoir by the capillary action of the wick fibres.

The incandescent mantle was developed in 1885. One disadvantage of this kind of lamp was its unsuitability for use in a portable lantern, the movement of the reservoir causing a surge in the supply of oil which resulted in excess carbon deposit. A lamp burning gasified oil was developed in Sweden in 1881 and a more sophisticated version for export was developed by 1902. Vaporization could not take place without first heating the supply tube, initially by a tray of methylated spirits and then sustained by arranging the supply tubes close to the mantle. The old style Argand burner remained in use until the 1960s.

## Gas burners

The first coal-gas fuelled lighthouse was lit at Salvore, near Trieste, in 1818. In the same year proposals were made to light the tower on Flatholm by a curious candelabrum in the shape of a ship's anchor outlined in gas-jets.

At Holyhead, Rennie's delightful little tower, built with the pier c.1820, was lit by oil gas. Here, alas, all was not well with the system. In one year there were three separate explosions, resulting in one fatality. An explosion reported in 1834 might have been anticipated as the repairer had approached the faulty and allegedly empty gasholder with a lighted candle.

The costs of transporting supplies of coal to remote lighthouses discouraged the general use of coal-gas except at those sites where it was possible to use town gas. However several cases were noted when the gasburners of lighthouses were discovered extinguished at times of peak domestic demand! Town coal-gas was used extensively for small harbour lights but was generally displaced by vaporizing paraffin oil.

By 1992 three Welsh lighthouses remained powered by acetylene gas: Caldy, Trwyn-du and St. Tudwal's, but the latter will be the only unelectrified light in Wales by 1995.

## Electric lights

Trinity House used electric light at Dungeness in 1862 but at this time it was expensive and labour intensive. The generators were belt-driven by steam engines which demanded not only a shift of stokers but also the carriage of fuel and the provision of boiler-feed and condensing water reservoirs. Gradually of course the economics of using electric light improved and by 1992 all the lamps at functioning lighthouses in Wales had been strengthened and updated and are lit by electricity, except for Caldy, St. Tudwals and Trwyn-du which, as said, are powered by acetylene gas. Land-based lighthouses are powered by mains electricity with a generator standby and offshore lighthouses have their own permanently operational generators. Caldy is scheduled to be electrified by 1994. The future source of power may be indicated by Trwyn-du which is due to be converted to solar power in 1993.

## Optics

The simple light produced by whatever source of illumination had usually to be concentrated and directed. Simple reflectors, hyperbolic reflectors and the ensembles of lenses surrounded by successive rings of triangular prisms are simplistically categorised under the following terms:

*Catoptric:* the use of mirrors to reflect the light outwards to sea.

*Dioptric:* the use of refraction, or the deflection of light-rays by a glass lens.

*Catadioptric:* This usually consists of a central main lens surrounded by reflective glass prisms (triangular bars of glass) to project all the light horizontally out to sea. Occasionally mirrors also reflect the light outwards.

The evolution of lighthouse optics is a splendid example of the realization of brilliant scientific theory by superb craftsmen. It seems that reflectors were first used in the Baltic, as early as 1532, and by the late seventeenth century it was realized that the parabola was the most efficient shape.

Britain lagged behind in the use of reflectors, but by 1763 metal reflectors were adopted which were lined with fragments of mirror glass set in plaster, rather like the stones in a Roman mosaic pavement.

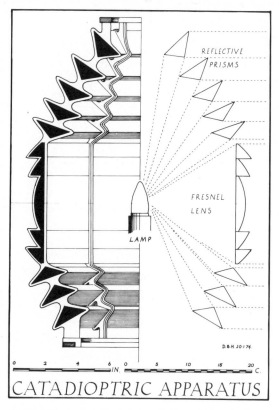

REFLECTIVE PRISMS

FRESNEL LENS

LAMP

D.B.H. 20·1·74.

0   2   4   6 0   5   10   15   20
IN.                              C.

# CATADIOPTRIC APPARATUS

*Simplified cross-section showing the Fresnel lenses in the centre of the optic. Reflective glass prisms (triangular bars of glass) caught the light rays and projected them seawards.*

As the source of light is not, like a laser, a point, but an area of considerable size, a great many reflected rays were ex-focal and diverged. Yet it was this very fault, the divergence of a beam over a distance, which made it so suitable for revolving lights.

Most reflectors were of silver-plated copper, and considerable numbers were used. At Bardsey, in 1823, there were three tiers, the upper two having five reflectors each, while the lower tier of reflecting lights had six. Small sector-lights used metal reflectors until quite recently. Lighthouse lanterns are superb examples of design and craftsmanship both in optics and mechanical engineering, and it is sad that with the coming of automation, the privilege of seeing them will be limited to very few.

In the middle of the eighteenth century, several attempts were made to fit large convex lenses in the lanterns of lighthouses, but none was satisfactory.

The difficulties involved exercised several opticians, notably Buffon and Condercet. It was a French scientist, the polymath Augustine J. Fresnel (1788-1827), who invented and fully understood the complex annular lens. The construction of this involved subtle changes in the profile of concentric rings of glass. The basic idea is that of a glass cage made of the central lens surrounded by rings of glass set one within another in an oval metal frame. All rays of light that were previously wasted on the floor and roof of the lantern were redirected into a ring of broad level beams by these rings of triangular glass prisms.

Sometimes the powerful beams produced by these optics remain as a fixed light but more often than not they are individually designed and the concentrated beams rotate to produce a recognizable signal of identification. The framework or cage supporting the glass is fixed to a circular iron platform. This, although fixed by a series of steel rollers, floats freely in a trough of mercury which provides an almost frictionless bearing, capable of being turned with one finger. Roller-bearings would have been quickly worn by the large weight of the complex optics and this idea of a turntable floating in a huge bath of mercury was developed by the famous mathematician, Dr John Hopkinson, working with the lighthouse specialist, Sir James Timmins Chance.

Rotative power used to be provided by some of the most beautiful clockwork mechanisms ever made, with a heavy weight falling within a central tube. Depending on the height of a tower, the weight might have to be wound several times during a night watch. At Maughold Head on the Isle of Man, where the tower was sited above an old mineshaft, an extra long cable was provided for the weight.

Despite the advent of motors, the old clockwork machinery has, in many cases, been retained for emergencies, serving as a monument to an age when craftsmanship flourished and was too precious to be trammelled by financial expediency. It is sad, however, that there have been cases of modernization where the old optic has been replaced by a sealed-beam unit, which is little more than a battery of car headlamp units mounted on a revolving box.

In Wales the optics have generally been retained,

*A catadioptric apparatus in situ. with a shallow convex mirror above. A vertical tube underneath encased the clockwork mechanism and counterweights for rotating the apparatus on rollers (Trinity House).*

# BARDSEY
# LIGHTHOUSE

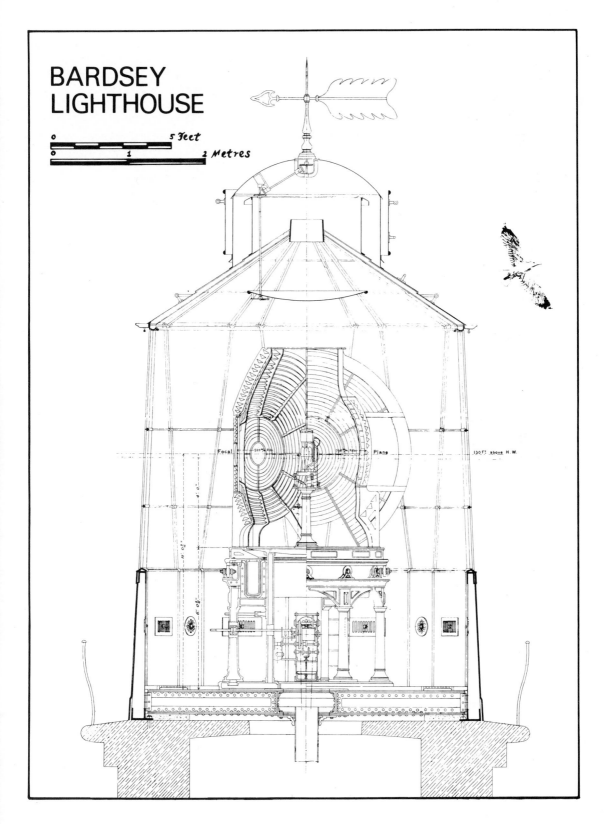

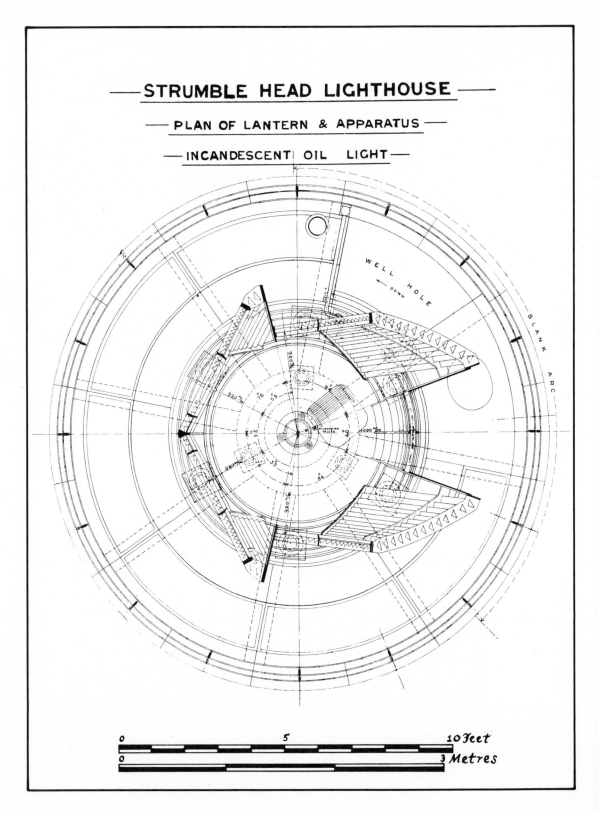

# — STRUMBLE HEAD LIGHTHOUSE —

## — PLAN OF LANTERN & APPARATUS —

## — INCANDESCENT OIL LIGHT —

with some modification, and are now all powered by electricity. However by 1979 the original complex optics had been replaced by sealed units at Mumbles, Saundersfoot Harbour and Llanddwyn Island Lighthouses.

Many of the optics used in British lighthouses, and many overseas, were oil-burning units with revolving lenses supplied by Chance Brothers glassworks in the Black Country, near Birmingham.[8] In the mid twentieth century some optics have been replaced or updated by this manufacturer's successors - *'Stone Chance'* of Crawley.

In a manned lighthouse, of which only two were left in Wales by 1992, the keeper who extinguished the light each morning hung curtains to prevent the sun's rays from being concentrated and causing a fire. With automation this danger has been countered by keeping the light burning continuously.

The 1862 dioptric optic from the Great Orme's Head Lighthouse can now be inspected at the Visitors' Centre on the Great Orme in Llandudno in Gwynedd, together with the bulb-changer and timing mechanism from the light. This was last used on 22 March 1985.[9]

# Lantern construction

Where the lantern was glazed all round, the entire weight of the roof had to be carried on the glazing bars which were therefore of sturdy cross-section. In the exposed situations in which lighthouses were sited it was necessary to provide bracing struts as are even found on the medieval French lantern at Aigues Mortes. These braces rose from the gallery floor and curved upwards to meet the glazing bars just below the eaves of the lantern and were usually four in number. They became very popular in the early nineteenth century, but only one example survives on the lighthouses run by Trinity House. Another good example survives at the disused lighthouse off Point of Ayr in Flintshire. The need for windbraces disappeared in the mid nineteenth century with the introduction of diagonal glazing bars by James Douglass and the Stevensons. This gave lateral bracing that could resist strong winds. It also eliminated the obstruction or interruptions in

*Cross-section of a lantern and optic showing the position of the frames holding the reflective glass prisms. The position of the iron columns holding the optic is shown by the circles underneath (Trinity House).*

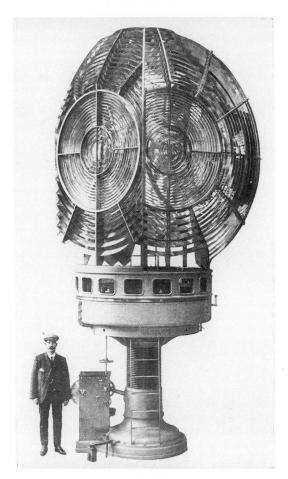

*Catadioptric apparatus produced at the Chance Brothers Lighthouse Works in West Bromwich, near Birmingham, pictured in 1925 before dispatch to China.*

the broadcast beam caused by the vertical glazing bars, particularly significant when fixed lights were in use. Salt Island, Holyhead, retains one of the few examples of early cast-iron lighthouse balcony railings.

---

[8] For a history of Chance Brothers *see* J.F. Chance, *A History of the firm of Chance Brothers & Co.* (London, 1919). Chance's Glassworks, Spon Lane, West Bromwich (SP 005 897) was famous for its 'Lighthouse Works' set up to manufacture Fresnel-type optics which were exported all over the world. Mid nineteenth-century offices and canal-side warehouses still survive on the glassworks site (J. Crompton, ed., *A Guide to the Industrial Archaeology of the West Midland Iron District* (Ironbridge, 1991).

[9] Verbal information, Mr. Callin, the present owner of the old Great Orme's Head Lighthouse.

Within the last two decades, progress has been made in the structural use of various plastics and glass-fibre, and whole towers of flanged tube units can be flown by helicopter to difficult sites and bolted to a concrete foundation.

# Fog signals

The use of sound signals as a warning in fog must have been common practice from antiquity. The first known drawing of a fog signal dates from 1766, and in Britain from 1777 a navigation bell, augmented by a cannon, was sounded from Bamburgh Castle, Northumberland. At South Stack, Holyhead, a two-ton inverted bell was used, although this was much less penetrating than the cannon which, in heavy fog, were fired from the high cliff behind the island and were audible on the Skerries, 14.5km (9 miles) away. Tedious manually-operated explosive signals were used in such remote rock towers as the Smalls (Pembrokeshire) where space was very limited. Small Tonite charges had to be attached to a jib on the lantern gallery and, when elevated, fired electrically. This was an unpleasant duty on a foggy winter's night, and at some stations the timing of the explosions gave the keeper little time to handle the apparatus. The signal had the disadvantage of a limited range. Compressed air signals were also used from the 1850s. Electrical diaphragm emitters replaced some of these. Radio beacons, at some lighthouses outside Wales, have to some extent supplanted visual and sound signals. Fog-horns on many Welsh lighthouses (including the specialised fog-warning station at North Stack, Holyhead) have been phased out over the last few years with the introduction and more extensive use of accurate position-fixing equipment, like 'Decca' and 'Satnav' by sea-going vessels, and the use of radar by large ships.

# Telegraph systems

The provision of lighthouses was only one of the several functions provided for the safety and convenience of mariners and ship-owners by the local trustee, or powerful port authority, as owners of lighthouse stations. Multi-function lighthouse settlements often housed pilot and lifeboat facilities. Liverpool, the pre-eminent commercial port of Britain outside London in the nineteenth-century, paralleled the greatest naval port, Portsmouth, in having a specialist telegraph system to carry news of

shipping movements across country at incredible speeds for the contemporary age. In 1810 the merchants of Liverpool set up a signalling station on Holyhead Mountain, and this was supplemented between 1826 and 1829 by a complete chain of signals to carry messages by way of Point Lynas, Puffin Island, the Great Orme, Llysfaen and Point of Ayr to Chester and Liverpool. By means of these *'telegraphs'* (each consisting of a mast with six arms working a system of code signals - one of the stations on the Portsmouth to London system has recently been restored to working order) news of the arrival and departure of vessels could be sent from one end of the chain to the other, taking on clear days less than a minute. Life-saving apparatus was also provided on the coast of north Wales (at Point Lynas, the Great Orme and Point of Ayr) by order of the House of Commons in 1815.[10]

# Lighthouse-keepers and their dwellings

The first lighthouses often had insufficient room and facilities to attract the first keepers and their families who were supposed to be attending the vital lights. The light at Point of Ayr, for example, first shone on 30 September 1777. Its keeper was a Mr. Edward Price who had been recommended by the influential landowner Sir Pyers Mostyn. No separate dwellings were provided and the keeper's family was expected to share the three rooms of the tower (*see* drawing) above the coal-cellar with the lighthouse stores. Perhaps not surprisingly, the commissioners of the light soon became aware that the keeper was not residing at the lighthouse with his family. He was called to Chester and warned to live in the lighthouse and to carry out his work as agreed. To encourage him the lighthouse committee decided to pay him £18 per annum instead of his existing salary of £16 16s 0d.[11]

By contrast, the early eighteenth-century detached keeper's house on the Skerries provided more spacious living room and may be the first such

*Fog frequently obscured the light at the South Stack, Holyhead, and a mobile lantern was built to show a light below the level of the fog (G. H. Elliot 1873).*

---

[10]A.H. Dodd, *The Industrial Revolution in North Wales* (Cardiff, 1971), 123.

[11]G.I. Hawkes, 'The Point of Ayr Lighthouses', *Cymru a'r Mor: Maritime Wales* **9** (1985), 32-43.

*The early eighteenth-century keeper's house on the Skerries flanked by sections of the narrow-gauge railways from the loading-jetties.*

residence ever built. Its crow-stepped gables mirror the traditions of well-built vernacular architecture on Anglesey.

On isolated rock lighthouses there was no room to build detached accommodation and the pioneering character of the Smalls Lighthouse, built in 1775-77, was likened to the appearance of a 'Barracoon' - a building constructed on wooden stilts and intended for the reception of slaves. The single room below the lantern was an octagon 6.7m (22ft) in width and eventually to accommodate two lighthouse keepers, the lighthouse master and stores.[12]

The Smalls and all other sea-girt towers were alleged to have been compelled to have a three-man staff always in residence after a bizarre event in the early nineteenth century. One of a pair of lightkeepers on the Smalls died of natural causes. The two

men, Thomas Griffith and Thomas Howell, had only just commenced a new turn of duty when Griffith died after a very short illness. The surviving man, Thomas Howell, was fearful lest he be accused of a murder and the wretched man felt obliged to preserve the corpse. This he did by making a rough coffin in which he placed his colleague, then with great difficulty he managed to hang it from the gallery to await the arrival of relief. Unfortunately this was delayed by bad weather, by which time the poor man was almost demented.

The conditions of work on such an isolated and pioneering structure could be extremely hazardous. The great gales of 18-19 October 1812 certainly meant that the Smalls lighthouse keepers merited their £30 a year pay. During the first night of the storm, the breakwater protecting the foot of the supporting oak pillars of the lighthouse gave way and the western two of the nine pillars were smashed out of place. This seriously damaged the floor of the living accommodation as the supports tore away from its underside. The windows were blown in and *'The lanthorn* (i.e. the lantern) *was entirely destroyed'*. The keepers penned an S.O.S. letter to the engineer/agent at Solva and dispatched it in a wooden cask. This was picked up on the Pembrokeshire coast some days later but the continued foul weather prevented rescue until 8 November. The crew had spent their last few days on the ruined structure huddled in a corner of the battered and creaking upper room which was held together with rusty nails and driftwood having survived for twenty-one days on a diet of bread and cheese. This had not been the only parlous time for the lighthouse-keepers or the only occasion when casks with notes had been dispatched to the shore. However after 1812 the more adequately funded Trinity House took over the lighthouse and repaired it soundly enough for it to last until the great stone tower was built in 1861.

By contrast most lighthouse stations, when sited on the mainland or on considerable islands, consist of buildings, often finely-grouped and detailed, that have evolved over 150 years or more. The buildings

*The traditional circular design of the lighthouse has been the model for the development of lighthouse stations planned as a series of sweeping areas and curves. Here they also enclosed a telegraph room and twin dwellings (Trinity House).*

---

[12]E. Freeman, *The Solva Saga* (Llanblethian, 1958), 5-9.

# Great Ormes Head Lighthouse

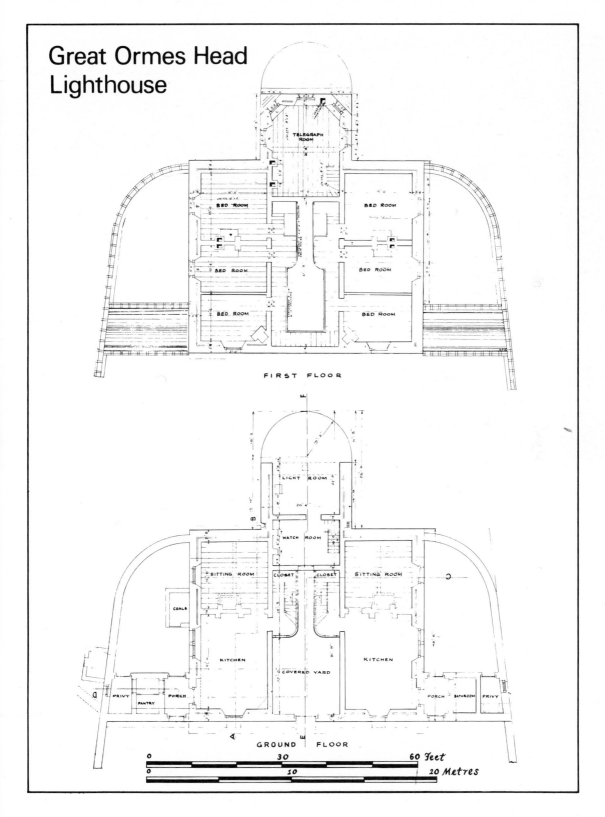

FIRST FLOOR

GROUND FLOOR

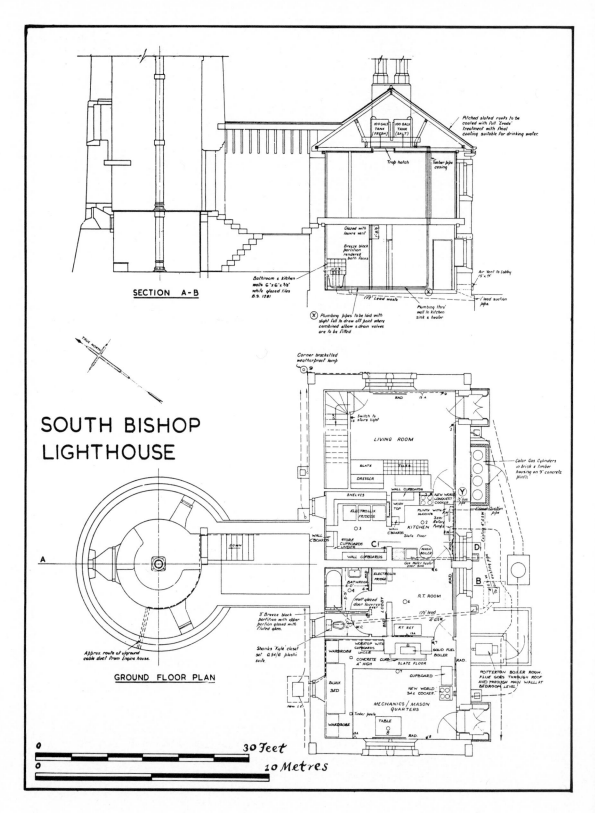

SECTION A-B

SOUTH BISHOP
LIGHTHOUSE

GROUND FLOOR PLAN

30 Feet

10 Metres

comprise multifarious stores, dwellings for the families of light-keepers, and an assortment of other accretions. Jeremy Lowe's work on the census records of the lighthouse community near the twin lighthouses at Nash Point, Glamorgan, has revealed something of their nature.[13] One of the four single-storeyed, pyramidally roofed, lighthouse cottages, built with their central chimney-stacks surrounded by four heated rooms was completed next to the contemporary western or lower lighthouse in 1832. In one room of the four there was a large (cooking) hearth and two external doorways: one of them later connected to a secondary corridor leading directly into the western, or low, lighthouse. There was only one keeper at first, for it was common for heavy responsibilities to be laid on one lowly-paid working man. In 1841 he was Rees

Palmer, a 45-year-old widower with four teenage children. By 1851 duties were shared between three keepers and a second centrally-planned cottage was added alongside the first in characteristic Trinity House symmetry. The principal keeper in 1851 was 30-year-old Daniel Daniels, who lived here with his wife Mary and their two baby sons. They also had an 18-year-old servant, Sarah Robert.

These more comfortable lighthouse stations obviously engendered a lighthouse community that had shared links and relationships throughout Wales. Mrs Hughes-Evans, the descendant of one of the families involved in this community, sent a letter

---

[13]J. Lowe, *Welsh Country Workers Housing, 1775-1875* (Cardiff, 1985), 23.

*Many of the lighthouse dwellings have retained their basic form despite constant upgrading and the ending of permanent occupation. These granite houses, originally built as twin dwellings in 1838-39, are connected to the light-tower by a covered passage; it was a feature common to many lighthouse stations. The bedrooms connect directly to the foot of the ascent to the light itself (Trinity House).*

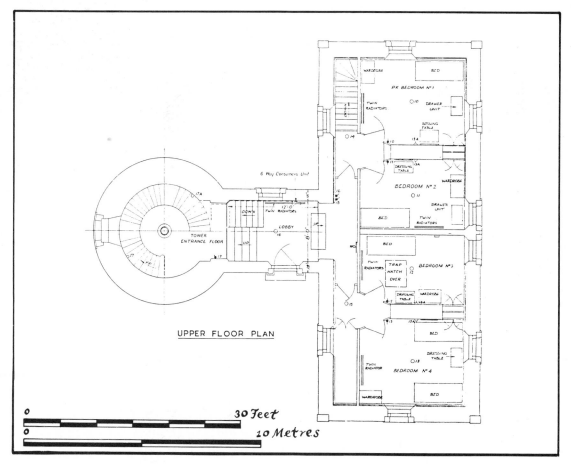

UPPER FLOOR PLAN

*Lighthouse-keepers, lifeboat-men and pilots lived in this row of cottages on Llanddwyn Island, Anglesey. They were built by a local Trust and were unlike the symmetrical houses constructed by Trinity House.*

to the press in the 1960s in which she related how her grandmother's uncle was keeper at the Point of Ayr Lighthouse for forty-eight years in the late eighteenth and early nineteenth centuries. Her grandmother's uncle adopted Mrs Hughes-Evan's grandmother when her great-grandmother died; they were then at the South Stack Lighthouse, at Holyhead. Her grandmother's sister was sent to the Skerries Lighthouse, off Anglesey, to be brought up.[14]

Those cottages adjoining lighthouses not built by Trinity House were much less likely to have a symmetrically planned layout and were more likely to conform with local building traditions. The detached early eighteenth-century lightkeeper's cottage on the Skerries, with its crow-stepped gables, is probably the earliest such detached lightkeeper's cottage in the world.

The single-storey Pilots' Cottages alongside the

lights on Llanddwyn Island (Anglesey) are of the traditional *croglofft* type with a main living-room the height of the cottage and a sleeping loft, accessible by ladder, over the subsidiary unheated chamber (the main bedroom) and pantry. A row of four of these cottages housed the families of the pilots who took sailing ships between shifting sandbanks to the ports of Caernarfon and Y Felinheli (Port Dinorwic). This same community also presumably tended the lighthouse and manned the lifeboat. The houses on this tidal island were built in the nineteenth century and are now open to the public and also house craft workshops.[15] A large communal privy was built over a substantial cess-pit cut into the rock

[14]G.I. Hawkes, 'The Point of Ayr Lighthouses', *Cymru a'r Mor: Maritime Wales* **9** (1985). 32-43.
[15]J. Lowe, *Welsh Country Workers Housing, 1775-1875* (Cardiff, 1985), 24-5.

behind the row of houses and two outhouses lie at the end of the row.

Some details of this still-picturesque combined lighthouse, pilot and lifeboat settlement are known from the minutes of the managing trustees. By December 1830 a pilot and lifeboat station was maintained on Llanddwyn Island, the men living in the cottages on site. The cottages were extensively repaired in 1852 and again in 1886; the privies were built in September 1861. The trustees had applied for financial support for maintaining the light in 1859 and in the 1860s money was available for the general improvement of the settlement. In 1865 the construction of an embanked roadway between Llanddwyn and Anglesey was begun, the Royal National Lifeboat Institution contributing £15. However in August 1887 the pilots were refused the opportunity of augmenting their income by keeping lodgers. In November 1894 the isolation of this life-saving settlement was alleviated by the connection of a telephone to the senior pilot's cottage. In February 1943 the pilot station was withdrawn and the process of depopulation began.

Various other buildings stood on the site. In June 1838 a breakwater had been constructed, and in July 1840 the trustees spent £30 building a new boathouse. In May 1916 repairs to the boathouse were carried out and in September 1938 the two boathouses then existing at Llanddwyn were repaired at a cost of £22.

Drinking water on island lights was often provided by rainwater collection tanks rather than wells descending to saline depths. However, the Skerries lighthouse settlement includes a pretty covered well.

Nash Point (Glamorgan) and St. Ann's (Pembrokeshire) were the only lights that remained manually operated along the Welsh coast in 1992 (Lundy Island, South, situated far out in the Bristol Channel towards Devon, is also still manned). With the control centre at Holyhead, they operate other lighthouses in their designated areas. The keepers at Nash Point now control the unmanned lighthouses on Flatholm Island, at Mumbles and the light-float at Breaksea (SS 093 610). The keepers at St. Ann's control the unmanned island and rock lights at Skokholm, South Bishop and on the Smalls. The Holyhead control centre operates the South Stack and Breakwater lights at Holyhead, Point Lynas, and the remote island lights at Bardsey and on the Skerries. Gone are the days when the courtyards, homes and towers of this widely dispersed, but close-knit lighthouse community echoed to the cries of the children and families of now long-gone keepers. Most of the rather elegant cottages are no longer lived in by keepers and have been leased or sold to conservation trusts or other occupants, but still offer overnight shelter to present-day lighthouse-keepers on their maintenance tours from the three regional control points or the Trinity House depot at Swansea. It is even possible to stay in the privately occupied lighthouses at Great Orme's Head, Llandudno and West Usk, Newport. The silence of the working lighthouses at Strumble Head (an automatic light), Caldy Island and East Usk is still disturbed by the visits of non-residential attendants.[16]

# Light-vessels

In many locations with hidden dangers it was impossible, or too expensive, to build permanent light-towers. In these locations light-vessels were in use from the early eighteenth century. Around 1820 anchorage chains became more available and reliable, and with the assurance of more secure anchorages, purpose-made light-vessels were designed and built. These are engine-less and are towed into position. By 1875 three light-vessels were in use off the coasts of Wales: one in Caernarfon Bay, a second off Cardigan, and a third off Worms Head in Gower.

*Vessel No 44* had her first mooring in Caernarfon Bay in December 1869. Her teak hull is 32m long, of 7m beam and 2.28m draught. Since 1945 she has been used as a club-house by the Erith Yacht Club in Kent. There is an iron deck-house and it is believed that her iron mast, now removed, carried the first revolving lantern to be used on a British light-vessel.

Until fairly recently there were still three manned light-vessels moored off the coast of south Wales. One of these, the steel-hulled light-vessel *'Helwick'*, formerly marking the Helwick Bank (at SS 323 808), can now be visited as one of the exhibits in the Swansea Maritime and Industrial Museum. The *'Scarweather'* was moored off Port Talbot (SS 659 744) and is also preserved - at the *Musée des Bateaux, Douarnenez, Brittany*. The *'St. Gawan'*, off St. Govan's Head in Pembrokeshire (SS 919 829) is still in active use, as is the unmanned light-float *'Breaksea'*.

---

[16]Personal communication, Jane Wilson of Trinity House, London.

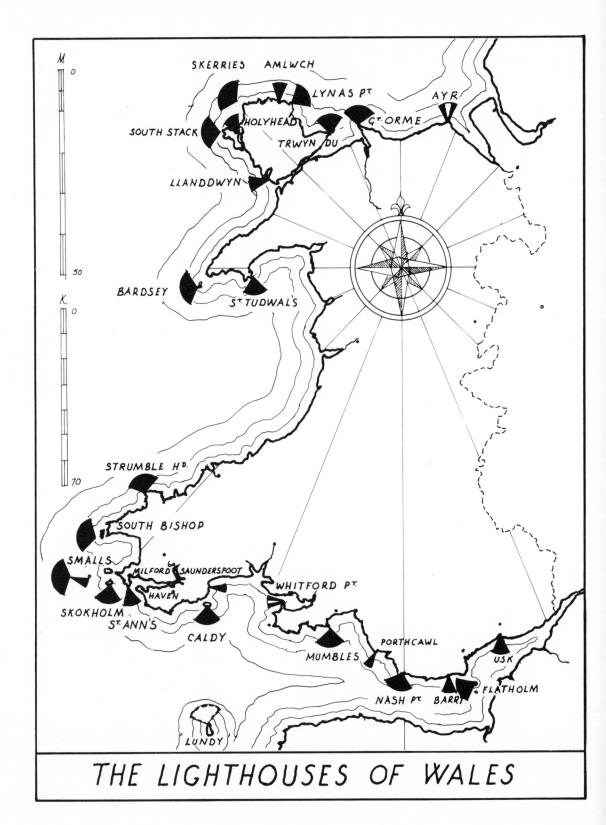

# THE LIGHTHOUSES OF WALES

M
0
50

K.
0
70

SKERRIES    AMLWCH
LYNAS Pᵀ
AYR
HOLYHEAD    Gᵀ ORME
SOUTH STACK
TRWYN DU
LLANDDWYN
BARDSEY
Sᵀ TUDWAL'S
STRUMBLE Hᴰ.
SOUTH BISHOP
SMALLS
MILFORD    SAUNDERSFOOT
HAVEN
WHITFORD Pᵀ
SKOKHOLM
Sᵀ ANN'S
CALDY
PORTHCAWL
MUMBLES
USK
NASH Pᵀ  BARRY  FLATHOLM
LUNDY

# Lighthouse buildings in Wales

The following descriptions of Lighthouses in Wales include the more significant and substantial structures. Various minor lights such as the 3.7m (12ft) high circular brick tower at Price Point on the Menai Straits, and some of the many harbour lights, are not included. The most significant sites described here are arranged in an anticlockwise direction from north-east to south-east Wales and can be followed easily on the accompanying map. The Royal Commission would be grateful for additional information on these and other sites.

All the surviving lighthouse towers can clearly be seen from the outside. The increasing reliability of automatic mechanisms, and in remote control, is resulting in more stations becoming unmanned with a consequent threat to all the elaborate structures once required to maintain a manned lighthouse station. Ultimately the ever widening use of locational radar may undermine the economic justification for the maintenance of any lights. These wonderful monuments of functionalism, a key to the spread of the world's first Industrial Revolution across the globe, are all likely to face some searching questions about the continued justification for maintaining the dwellings, stores, elaborate optics and superb lighthouse structures that comprised the eighteenth-, nineteenth- and twentieth-century structures that form such an aesthetically pleasing and yet historically significant heritage.

In the following inventory of sites lighthouses have been graded according to their historical, architectural and engineering significance:

**** Buildings and/or fittings of international importance

*** Buildings and/or fittings of British importance

** Buildings and/or fittings of importance within Wales

* Buildings and/or fittings of local importance

*The English and Welsh names of each site are followed by the present and historic county designation, and a six-figure Ordnance Survey grid reference.*

## Point of Ayr: Y Parlwr Du, Clwyd (Flint. SJ 121853) **

*This building is important because it retains one of the earliest lanterns in Wales.*

It was a landfall light marking the entrance to the treacherous Dee estuary. The small size of medieval ships allowed Chester, at the head of the difficult estuary, to grow into a very important port trading with the French wine ports, Dublin and the boroughs of the north Wales coast.[1] In 1562 the boundaries of the port extended from Barmouth as far as the River Duddon, below Carlisle. Liverpool was then only a creek of this port, but was of course to grow in the post-medieval period to become the pre-eminent port of western Britain. The lighting arrangements for the important medieval port of Chester are obscure, as is the date and function of the *'Pharos'* (*see* introduction) at Whitford Garn in Flintshire. Hilbre Island, on the Lancashire side of the mouth of the Dee, had a light by about 1236, for which the Earl of Chester paid 10s annually for its upkeep.[2]

---

[1]  K.L. Gruffydd, 'Maritime Dee during the Later Middle Ages', *Cymru a'r Mor: Maritime Wales* **9** (1985), 7-31.
[2]  G.I. Hawkes, 'The Point of Ayr Lighthouses', *Cymru a'r Mor: Maritime Wales* **9** (1985), 32-43.

*Point of Ayr Lighthouse has long ceased use but it retains one of the earliest lanterns in Wales.*

The bill for the canalization of the Dee in 1733 was designed to allow bigger vessels to safely enter Chester and to end the post-medieval decline of the port. The bill included proposals for a lighthouse but, as elsewhere, the powerful Liverpool lobby opposed further lights (probably because they neither wished to pay tolls from installations that did not directly guide the main flow of traffic into their pre-eminent port, or to revive the fortunes of their old competitor).[3] However the issue was given renewed impetus by the loss of two Dublin packets, the *Nonpareil* and the *Trevor*, in a north-westerly hurricane on October 19 1775 with the loss of over 200 lives and £46,000 worth of cargo. Ambitious plans by Chester merchants for two Point of Ayr Lighthouses and systems of buoys and landmarks were not supported by the Dee River Company on grounds of costs, and opposed by Liverpool merchants because, supposedly, mariners might confuse new lights with the existing ones on the Liverpool approaches. To reduce possible costs, the committee asked Mr. Turner, a well-known architect from Hawarden, to design a timber-built lighthouse that would top the surrounding hills by 9.1m (30ft). However, a new lighthouse was built modelled on the existing Liverpool Docks Board light at Hoylake and the base of the light bore the initials H.T. (Turner?). Detailed estimates for this light-tower, 16m (52ft) high and with an external diameter 7.8m (25.75ft) at the bottom and 4.9m (16ft) at the top, were prepared by William Hamilton and a Mr. Meredith. The total cost was estimated at £349 8s 1d (*see* the detailed copy of the accounts in the introduction).[4]

It has been claimed that the first lighthouse was built on a rock in the channel much further out than the present one,[5] and destroyed by the appearance of a large cavity under the foundations. However, the minutes of trustees do not mention the event, and the present dimensions of the height of the tower, and its three floors and basement coalstore seem to conform with those given in the original estimate of 1776. It can also be seen from the section that a considerable part of the top of the tower is contemporary with the 1820s lantern and post-dates

*The archaeology of this lighthouse confirms its early date.*

[3]   Ibid., 33.
[4]   'Estimate for Building a Lighthouse at Point of Ayre, Flints' (City of Chester Record Office, CB 165).
[5]   Hawkes, 38.

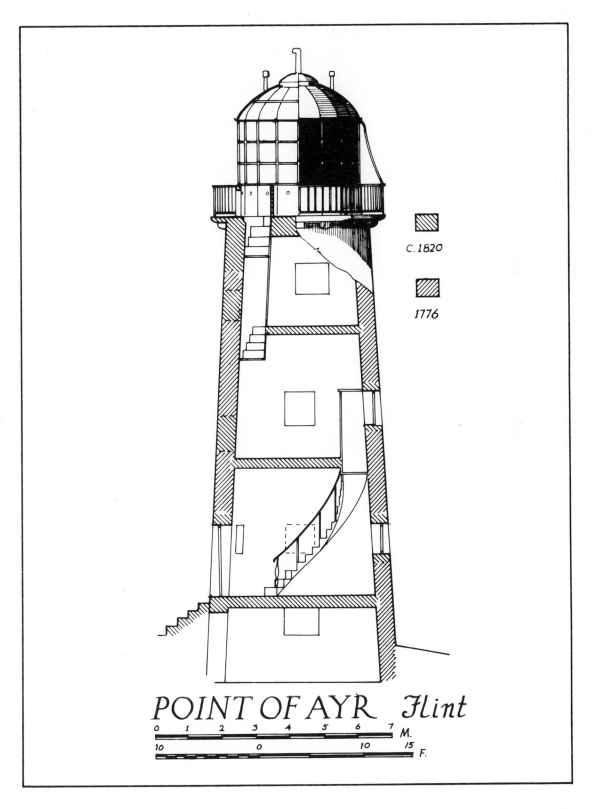

POINT OF AYR *Flint*

C.1820

1776

0 1 2 3 4 5 6 7 M.

10 0 10 15 F.

*The 1824 drawing by W. Latham clearly shows the present Point of Ayr Lighthouse lantern. (By permission of the National Library of Wales).*

the surviving earlier masonry of the tower. This rebuilding may well have followed a partial structural collapse recalled by a descendent of the lighthouse keeper 144 years after the event. The recent proposition that the present light was built by the eminent Scottish lighthouse engineer Robert Stevenson seems to confuse Point of Ayr with the similarly named Ayr Lighthouse in Scotland.[6] The dimensions given for his alleged design for the Welsh light-tower are no less than 30.2m (99ft) whilst the measurable height of the present lighthouse to the top of its lantern is only 17.7m (58ft). As will be seen elsewhere, it was standard practice for Trinity House to considerably improve and rebuild existing lights upon their assuming responsibility for an existing lighthouse station. Trinity House took over from the Point of Ayr Lighthouse trustees in 1819 and the lighthouse structure was much altered around 1820 (*see* the section) when the present lantern was fitted. What appears to be the existing 12m (40ft) high brick tower is well illustrated by W. Daniell in *c.*1810, and a good drawing by W. Latham in 1824 shows the surviving lantern and fenestration. The architect of the original tower was a Mr Turner, and his buildings accounts are some of the very few to survive. The light was directional, to the north and west only, and super-

---

[6]   Ibid., 39.

seded by a piled structure in 1844, since removed.

The piled light consisted of nine cast-iron cylinders sunk into the sand: a central support surrounded by eight outer stanchions. The piles were tied by two horizontal wrought-iron tension-rods arranged around their circumference, and by diagonal ties from the central post to each of the outer eight. The cabin for the keepers was a double-skinned structure capping the cast-iron legs. The outer part consisted of 'Palmer's patent corrugated iron plates', lined with boards on the inside. The cabin sat on top of a conical space occupied by a small kitchen and water closet and was itself capped by a lamp 'constructed of gun metal in a very superior manner.' The structure was designed by James Walker and Burges and made by Gordon and Co., of Deptford.[7]

Some of the 1840s piled-lights in the British Isles still survive but Point of Ayr had been replaced by a lightship moored to the north of the entrance to the Dee channels by December 1883. In 1891 a third Point of Ayr Lighthouse was built on the high water mark and was 10.4m (34ft) high.[8]

Today a light still shines out from Hilbre Island, Hoylake, on the Lancashire side of the mouth of the Dee (attended by a non-residential keeper).

# Great Orme's Head: Penygogarth,
## Gwynedd (Caernarfonshire. SH 756845) *

*An attractive building that was particularly important for the survival of its original telegraph equipment.*

The strong, square, castellated two-storey building is situated on the steep limestone cliffs of Great Orme's Head, 99m (325ft) above the sea. A letter from a K. Parker on the 3 December 1861, recorded in the Trinity House Minute Books, expressed the need for a lighthouse on the Great Orme which Trinity House approved. They decided that the optic should be dioptric, of the first order. It was designed and constructed by G. Lyster, engineer-in-chief to the Mersey Docks and Harbour Board (who also altered the Point Lynas Lighthouse in 1871). The light was first shown on 1 December 1862. It was Lyster's only design for a complete lighthouse. There had been a telegraph station in the vicinity, but no earlier light. The original light used paraffin wick-lamps, replaced in 1904 by vapourizing petroleum mantle-burners, superseded in 1923 by dissolved acetylene mantle-lamps producing 13,000 candle-power.[9]

As at Lynas, the lantern is at ground level with the signal and telegraph room above; the original equipment was still in place in 1979, carefully preserved by Trinity House, who had taken over the station. However the light shone for the last time on 22 March 1985 and lighthouse reverted to the Mersey Docks Company who sold the property. The telegraph equipment was taken away by the Docks Company.

The signal room on the north-western elevation of the lighthouse still retains telescope ports in its windows. The optic, bulb changer and timing

*The elaborate engineered siting of the Great Orme's Head Light*
*(N.M.R: Howarth-Loomes Collection).*

[7] Ibid., 41-2.
[8] Ibid., 42.
[9] Information from the Mersey Docks and Harbour Board Office; Marine surveyor and water bailiff, 15 November 1962.

mechanism can now be seen in the nearby Visitors' Centre.[10]

The south-eastern main elevation has a central doorway surmounted by a plaque which reads:

---

This lighthouse
was erected
by the Mersey Docks and Harbour Board
1862
C. F. Lyster, Engineer.

---

The doorway is flanked by wide bays with chamfered windows on both floors, surmounted by the machicolations of the castellated parapet. The sides of the lighthouse and its yards are enclosed by high blast-walls of massive construction similar to the rest of the building. The white rendering applied in 1974 has now been removed to reveal the limestone masonry of the structure, now a hotel.

*The linked twin dwellings on the Great Orme had a lantern projecting seawards
(N.M.R: Howarth-Loomes Collection).*

# Trwyn-du, Gwynedd (Anglesey. SH 644815) **

*This attractive and innovative tower by James Walker has a stepped base to discourage the huge upsurges of waves that had afflicted earlier towers and which also facilitated the downsurge from the first flushable lighthouse toilets.*

Set in the narrow strait between Penmon Point and Ynys Seiriol (Puffin Island), the tower marks the north entrance to the Menai Strait and the passage between the two islands. Although not a spectacular structure, it does display some innovations introduced by its designer James Walker. It was his first wave-washed tower, built in 1835-38,[11] and completed twenty years before his unsatisfactory Bishop, but similar to his Needles of 1859. He also designed the successful and famous Smalls of 1861 and Wolf Rock of 1870. At Trwyn-du he used a stepped base designed to discourage the upsurge by checking its force at the tower bottom. He also used austere vertical walls, not the conventional graceful lines of his Bishop and other rock towers, and this simplicity was clearly an economy measure. He narrowed the diameter of the tower upwards from the half-way point both here and on the Skerries (1846) and St Catherine's (1840) Lighthouses, but not on the Needles. Another characteristic feature of Walker's design, to be seen at these sites, is the use of crenellated or battlemented stone parapets in

preference to iron railings on the gallery. Finally a small matter of domestic planning: Walker pioneered the use of a primitive sort of water-closet by providing a specially designed drain leading out at the base of the tower. Unfortunately this device was not very successful, as under certain conditions an embarrassing upsurge of sea water was experienced. The tower has been unmanned for many years.

The continuous light at Trwyn-du is now checked from the Holyhead Control Centre and is due to be converted to solar power.

*James Walker's wave-washed Trwyn-du Lighthouse was a prototype for his more ambitious tower on the Smalls. A crenellated upper tower, similar to his Skerries Light, stands on a stepped base.*

---

10  Verbal information, Mr. Callin, the present owner of the Great Orme's Head Lighthouse.
11  Personal communication, Jane Wilson, Trinity House.

# Point Lynas, Gwynedd (Anglesey. SH 479936) ***

*This site is important for its association with Jesse Hartley, the famous engineer responsible for the robust innovative architecture of the world's first great floating-dock system at Liverpool.*

Point Lynas, together with Great Orme's Head, was built by the Mersey Docks and Harbour Board and this lighthouse, its most distant outpost, has only been taken over by Trinity House comparatively recently. Point Lynas was first established in 1779[12] at a site some 300m to the south of the present tower, primarily to provide suitable accommodation for the Liverpool pilots who could make use of the shelter of Porthyrysgaw. Two 0.28m (11ins) reflectors provided small lights which were displayed to the west and east. However, it became obvious that

a light was needed on the most important north-east quarter, but the high ground forming the headland made the use of the original site impossible for this purpose. In 1834 Alan Stevenson suggested that this difficulty could be overcome by building a 21m (70ft) high lighthouse tower, but it was finally decided to abandon the original site and erect a new tower on the present site to the north.[13]

Here, as the elevation of the natural ground

---

[12]   Marine Dept., Mersey Docks and Harbour Board.

*Point Lynas with its castellated square tower fronted by a ground-floor lantern, is immediately recognisable as one of the lighthouses designed for the Mersey Docks and Harbour Board.*

surface was already 39m, a light-tower was not required. The unusual arrangement of a lantern at ground level with the look-out and telegraph room above is similar to that on the summit of the Great Orme at Llandudno. The present romantic castellated building at Point Lynas was designed in 1835 by Jesse Hartley, engineer to the Mersey Docks and Harbour Board from 1824 to 1860, but with additions by G. Lyster some twenty years later. A two storey dwelling is surmounted by a square tower 11m (37ft) high. At the base of this was a projecting semicircular lantern 3.7m (12ft) in diameter protected by an external ditch. This silhouette with battlemented wall tops had the advantage of presenting an unusual and distinctive appearance from the sea. The lantern was flanked by a high wall which returned to the south to enclose a courtyard. It had a wall-walk carried on a series of internal arched recesses which is now inaccessible, but was probably reached from the southern curtain which was demolished around 1879; the site was about 13m (42ft) to the south of the front and is marked by two turrets which might have housed stairs (both contain evidence of blocked openings). The buildings are of rubble masonry, rendered and limewashed.

The present lantern is 4.6m (15ft) in diameter and dates from about 1874. A drawing of it preserved in the tower also gives details of the earlier arrangements. The square back of the present lantern is recessed behind a tall pointed arch which carries the front wall of the tower. This 3.5m (11ft 6ins) wide arch contains an iron column which supported the clockwork mechanism which gave the light its

13 Report in the records of the Mersey Docks and Harbour Board, dated 1834.

*The rear boundary of Point Lynas Lighthouse station was moved southwards in 1879 to accommodate two dwellings for staff operating the new telegraph; it was designed by George Lyster.*

*The lighthouse at Point Lynas with its lantern and pilot's look-out designed by Jesse Hartley.*

produced by boards which are turned by machinery; they turn slowly till their edges are towards the lamps, and then they close suddenly, and shut out the light. The machinery is wound by pulling an endless chain hand over hand rapidly. It takes the keeper 20 minutes to wind it, it goes for 4 hours. He says the labour is excessive 'killing'. It was tried and found to be severe....The reflectors were well polished, quite equal in that respect to any previously seen. They are 23 years old and are now much worn...The machinery, in particular, is very rude.'

A Chance occulting optic was fitted in 1878.[14] This is 1.4m (4ft 6ins) in diameter and displays a light through 206 degrees. The fixed part of the optic consists of three sections, the central unit on the focal plane has a 0.25m (10in) deep curved lens with bands of six prisms above and below it. The bottom unit is made up of six bands of reflective prisms, while the inclined top unit contains sixteen. The station was electrified in 1952 when chain, wires, pulleys and other working parts associated with the mechanical light-shutter were removed.

A telegraph station was established here in 1879 and two new cottages were erected to accommodate extra staff, necessitating the demolition of the old south wall of the courtyard. These dwellings are of red brick with limestone dressings, as is the wide two-centred arch spanning the entrance. The pointed top of the arch contains an inscribed tablet:

| ELIANUS POINT | |
|---|---|
| THIS LIGHTHOUSE ERECTED BY | |
| MERSEY DOCKS & HARBOUR BOARD | |
| | COTTAGES BUILT NEW |
| LIGHT FIRST EXHIBITED | LIGHT AND TELEGRAPH EST. |
| A 1835 D | A 1879 D |

In 1948 an automatic acetylene fog-gun was installed, but by 1973 this had been replaced by electrical emitters when the light was transferred to Trinity House. At that time it was planned that the new smaller pilot-boats might again be based at Porthyrysgaw. Point Lynas is now an automatic light controlled from Holyhead. Trinity House's lease of the lighthouse-keepers' dwellings was relinquished when the light was automated and occupation reverted to the owners: the Mersey Docks and Harbour Company.[15]

identifying characteristic by obscuring the beam for two seconds in every ten. One of the vapourizing lamps of this period survives. The lantern has a cast-iron lower wall and rectangular glazing bars take the wall height to some 3.7m (12ft), and is capped by a plain conical roof with ball finial. Corbelled out above the lantern is the bay or oriel window of the pilot's look-out. This consists of four vertical lights divided by horizontal bars (transoms), but the lower panes have been modified to accommodate large brass ball-joints to house telescopes, perhaps when Point Lynas became a telegraph station.

The arrangements of the original light-room caught the attention of the Commissioners when they visited the station during the preparation of the 1861 Report on Lighthouses and Buoys:

'The 13 lamps and reflectors are arranged on the inside of a curved frame, and placed in a bow window. The flash is

[14] Lighthouse Orders, 1 March, 1878 (Chance Brothers records, now at Stone Platt, Crawley).
[15] Personal communication, Jane Wilson, Trinity House, London.

# Amlwch, Gwynedd (Anglesey. SH 452937) ****

*The group significance of the features of the early copper-exporting port at Amlwch which served Parys Mountain makes the lighthouse part of a heritage site of international importance.*

The copper from Parys Mountain was exported from a small creek on the north-east tip of Anglesey. Following a private Act of 1793, the harbour was improved and two stubby piers built, each furnished with curious little octagonal houses apparently with small lanterns protruding from the roofs, described

*The dry-dock and lighthouse at Amlwch served the shipping of the largest copper-mine in Europe.*

47

*The outer pier at Amlwch was built in 1816 and the present lighthouse of 1853 is the fourth to serve this port. The lantern of this light was added later.*

in the *New Seaman's Guide* of 1821 as 'small white houses displaying lights at night'. In 1816 an outer pier some 46m (150ft) long was built to give extra protection to shipping inside the harbour. In the following year, this was furnished with a small lighthouse displaying a light at an elevation of 8.5m (28ft) above the high-water mark. This lighthouse rose 4.9m (16ft) from the surface of the pier and measured 4.6m (15ft) long by 3m (10ft) wide.

The present square tower with battered walls was erected in 1853. Its original fine ashlar masonry remains to a height of 15ft above which the present lantern of uncertain date has been added.

Fortunately the extensive works associated with the great off-shore oil terminal have not impinged on the attractive inner harbour.[16]

---

[16] For further information *see* J. Rowlands, *Copper Mountain* (Llangefni, 1981) 146-53.

# Skerries: Ynysoedd y Moelrhoniaid,
## Gwynedd (Anglesey. SH 268948) ***

*The early date of the detached keepers' cottage makes the buildings on this site of considerable interest.*

The Skerries are a small group of rocky islets off the north-west tip of Anglesey. Architecturally the buildings are not distinguished, although the attractive early eighteenth-century crow-stepped gabled cottage, 10m (33ft) by 5.2m (17ft), is certainly the oldest separate keepers' dwelling in the British Isles. The Skerries claim to distinction lies in its economic history which involved a remarkable rearguard action fought by its proprietors to protect their investment from a low take-over price by Trinity

*The wire ropeway at the Skerries Lighthouse was used for unloading boats. Behind this is the tower of the 1903 sector-light and behind this again the main lighthouse recased by James Walker c.1848.*

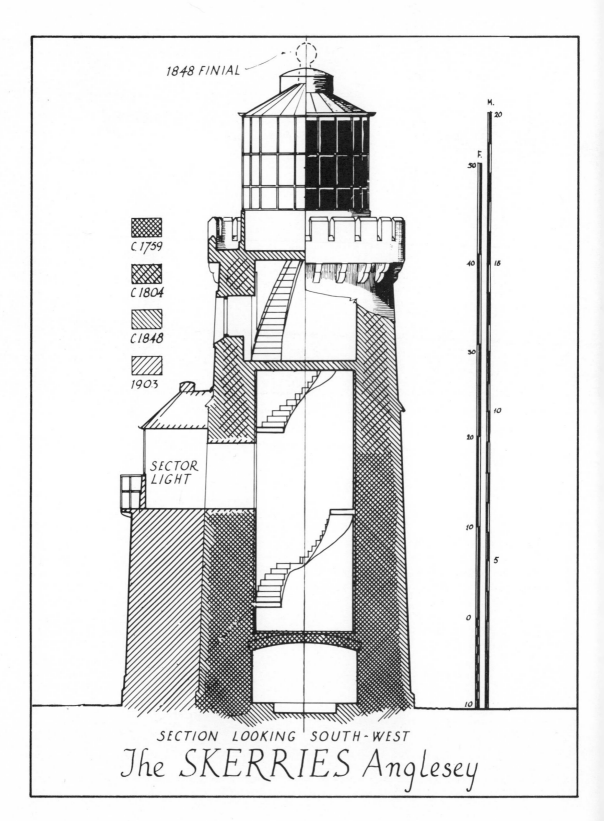

1848 FINIAL

C. 1759

C. 1804

C. 1848

1903

SECTOR
LIGHT

SECTION LOOKING SOUTH-WEST
The SKERRIES Anglesey

*The stone bridge connecting the Skerries augmented several landing places, railways and a cableway.*

House after their enabling Act of 1836. Eventually it was purchased for the record sum of £440,984 in 1844.

The lighthouse was established on the highest point of this group of rocky islands after 1716 and the builder, William Trench, is said to have originally been allowed a pension from Post Office revenue rather than payment from shipping tolls.[17]. A patent for the lighthouse was subsequently obtained in 1824.[18] This was a disastrous personal venture for Trench who lost his son off the rocks, and he died in debt in 1725. An Act of 1730 enabled his son-in-law, Sutton Morgan, to increase the dues charged to shipping and confirmed the patent on the light to Morgan's heirs forever. It was rebuilt by his heirs *c.*1759 for about £3,000 as a slightly tapering limestone tower 6.65m (21ft 10ins) in diameter and about 8.5m (28 ft) high, and was lit by a coal brazier on top of the tower. In 1778 the lighthouse was inherited by Morgan Jones, twice high sheriff of Cardiganshire, who in 1804 raised the top of the

*The castellated tower at the Skerries resembles James Walker's other tower at Trwyn-du but evolved over 150 years of successive rebuilding.*

tower by 6.7m (22ft) and built an iron balcony with railings enclosing the oil-burning lantern; the lantern was glazed all round with square panes and covered by a cupola.

After Trinity House had taken over the whole establishment, it was extensively restored by James Walker in a lavish style, possibly in keeping with its purchase price (paid to the executors of Morgan Jones II). The tower has a very slight taper and exhibits two of Walker's characteristics of design, a decrease in diameter and a solid parapet. A stone-built gallery 0.84m (2ft 9ins) wide is bracketed out on corbels with a crenellated parapet. A new cast-iron lantern, 4.25m (13ft 10ins) in diameter, was glazed with square panes around a dioptric light with mirrors. These 1851 mirrors have been replaced by a lens. The light shines out at a height of 36m (119ft) above high water. The grandiose layout includes well-protected cobbled yards for the castel-

[17]  A. Eames, *Ships and Seamen of Anglesey* (Anglesey, 1973), 321.
[18]  A.H. Dodd, *The Industrial Revolution in North Wales* (Cardiff, 1971), 123.

lated dwellings which are provided with entrance stairs, symmetrically sited privies with decorated doors, a garden, a stone bridge connecting two islets and a unique stone well-head building (this may, however, date from the early William Trench period). An axial corridor leads from the dwellings to the lighthouse tower base. In the tower there is an enigmatic circular anteroom with a moulded cornice which suggests an earlier roof. On the north side of the lighthouse tower is a former external doorway, exhibiting the Trinity House coat of arms, which now leads into the engine-room. Equally lavish were the curiously sited landing-places connected by narrow-gauge railways, and the harbour facilities also included unloading hooks suspended from pulleys operating on a wire ropeway (The 'Blondin' system more typical of the north Wales slate quarries).

Additions to the site include a solid circular tower, about 3m (10ft) in diameter, added to the south-west side of the tower in 1903-04 to carry a sector light, and more recently a helicopter pad has been built in one of the walled gardens.[19] The sector lantern shines out from an elevation of 26m (86ft) above the sea and has a diameter of 2.6m (9ft 2in). Access to the sector light is from an improvised landing in the main tower. The dwellings have been purged of embellishments, and later buildings, such as those connected with fog signals, have been arranged concentrically around the tower.

The remote Skerries Light is now automatic and controlled from Holyhead. However wardens from the Royal Society for the Protection of Birds have been resident in the keepers' cottages for the past few summers; a welcome use of these historic and attractive buildings.[20]

# Holyhead, Salt Island: Ynys Halen,
## Gwynedd (Anglesey. SH 256829) ***

*The structure merits national significance as a surviving work of John Rennie, one of the most eminent engineers of the world's first Industrial Revolution. Of particular significance in Wales is the early date of the lighthouse lantern.*

*Elegant curved railings crown Salt Island tower.*

This attractive ashlar tower, 14.6m (48 ft) high, was designed by the civil engineer John Rennie in 1821. It replaced an earlier tower illustrated by Daniel, the successor of a thatched structure of which unfortunately no more is known. Rennie also designed a matching tower at Howth in Ireland for the other terminal of the Irish packet. This neat, steeply battered tower was lit by gas. It was no longer used after the pier was extended. The tower has survived intact, preserving its lantern, probably the second oldest in Wales (after Point of Ayr), and beautiful curved gallery railings, which are very similar to those at Bardsey and Inner Farne. The end of the lengthened pier is marked by a light on a pole.

[19]  H.R. Davies, 'An Account of the Private Lighthouse of the Skerries', *Transactions of the Anglesey Antiquarian Society* (1924 & 1928); Trinity House plan. Report of the Select Committee on Lighthouses, *Parliamentary Paper*, 1845. Report from the Commissioners appointed to enquire into the Conditions and Management of Lights, Buoys and Beacons Parliamentary Paper, 1861.
[20]  Personal communication, Jane Wilson, Trinity House, London.

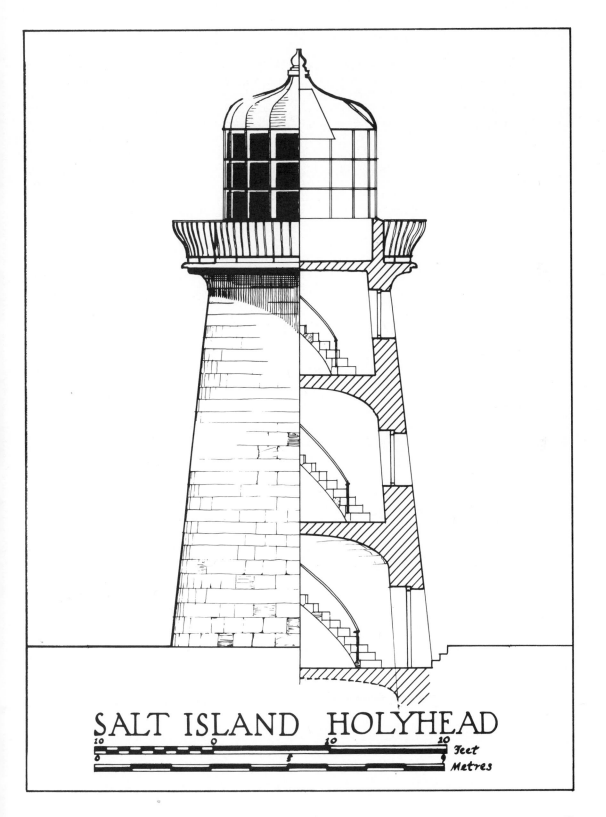

SALT ISLAND HOLYHEAD

10    0    10    20   Feet
0           5         Metres

*Rennie's monumental arch and fine tower (upper illustration), the latter replacing an earlier tower depicted by Daniell (lower illustration), the successor of a thatched structure.*
*(By permission of the National Library of Wales).*

# Holyhead Breakwater,
## Gwynedd (Anglesey. SH 257848) **

*This lighthouse is important as part of the ambitious engineering works of the harbour of refuge.*

It was erected at the end of the long breakwater protecting the harbour of refuge. The lighthouse was built between 1845 and 1873 and probably designed by John Hawkshaw, the superintendent engineer of the harbour works from 1857 to 1873. It is 19.2m (63ft) high with a roll-moulded string-course projecting above first floor level, and is unusual in being (6.78m - 22ft 3in) square in plan. A moulded cornice supports a walkway around the circular lantern and the domed apex is surmounted by a weather-vane and finial. This three-storeyed lighthouse is painted black and white with chamfered angles and a stepped plinth set on an oval platform on the breakwater. The lantern has inclined glazing bars.

Like most other lights in Gwynedd, this is now operated from the Holyhead Control Centre of Trinity House.

*Holyhead Breakwater Lighthouse.*

# South Stack, Gwynedd (Anglesey. SH 202823) **

*The remains of the unusual fog-light incline and the grouping of this fine set of functional structures in a spectacular setting contribute to the importance of this site.*

*At South Stack access was originally by a constructional cable-way and then a rope-bridge. (William Daniell - 1813. by permission of the National Library of Wales).*

The South Stack lighthouse occupies a site of dramatic grandeur on the 30.5m (100ft) summit of a small island off the north-west of Holyhead Island. Since the 27.7m (91ft) high lighthouse was erected in 1809, the scene has attracted and inspired countless artists, photographers and geologists. The 122m (400ft) high 'mainland' cliffs display fantastic and flamboyant folds of pre-Cambrian rocks. During the building operations a cable way was used to carry materials from the mainland to the island and in 1828 this and an early rope bridge were replaced by a suspension bridge (at a cost of £1,046), which in its

*The electronic fog signal at Holyhead South Stack replaced a compressed-air horn which had in turn replaced an inverted fog-bell and cannon.*

turn has been succeeded by a rigid tubular lattice-type bridge. Both lie at the foot of a spectacular descent of 400 stone steps. The engineer and builder of the tower were Daniel Alexander and Joseph Nelson respectively. Nelson later designed several more lighthouse towers on the west coast of Britain. The cost was £11,828 exclusive of the attendant dwellings also built by Nelson. Revolving Argand lamps and reflectors were added in 1818. In 1874 the white-painted tower was heightened and a new lantern fitted. The simple, dignified, and whitened tower is dominated by its atypical cornice with modillions (projecting brackets). An unknown artist painted two versions of an excellent view showing the tower under construction with rock being carried from the cliff top.

The site had two unusual features, an inverted fog-bell weighing 2.5 tons and an ingenious arrangement whereby, when the frequent fog or low cloud obscured the light, a small clockwork operated (3.05m (10ft) square) lantern mounted on wheels was lowered down a quarry-like railed incline to within 15.2m (50ft) of the sea. The builder and engineer of this early (1832) traveller-incline, cut into the north side of the rock, was a Hugh Evans.[21]

Only the bed of the incline survives today. A compressed-air horn was later fitted on this site and this in turn has been replaced by the fitting of an electronic fog signal.

The lighthouse was converted to automatic operation in 1984 and is operated from the Holyhead Control Centre. The former Trinity House Fog Signal Station at Holyhead North Stack has now also been sold off.[22]

# Llanddwyn Island: Ynys Llanddwyn,
Gwynedd (Anglesey. SH 385625) *

*A windmill builder may have designed Llanddwyn.*

An unusual coastal light first exhibited on 1 January 1846 from a rock at the west end of the tidal island marking the western entrance to the Menai Strait. The light was shown from a lantern at the foot of a tapering tower, 10.7m (35ft) high and 5.5m (18ft) in diameter, which may have been used previously as a day-mark. The tower has the considerable taper characteristic of the numerous Anglesey windmills and presumably a mason experienced in this work may have been employed here, assuming the tower was not originally used as a windmill. The cost of the lantern and fittings was £250 7s 6d which included the adaption of the 'earlier tower'. The present lantern window is some 2m (6ft 6ins) by 0.61m (2ft) and presumably is primary to the building. The optic, silver plated reflector and Fresnel lens, used into the 1970s, were dated 1861 and was originally lit by six Argand lamps with reflectors.[23] The northeast door of the tower is flanked by small windows; the two floors above were lit by windows but a considerable space at the top of the tower shows no signs of ever having had openings. The top is covered by a conical slate roof with flag-pole.

*The ground-floor lantern at Llanddwyn was attached to the earlier (Daymark?) tower.*

[21] *English Lighthouse Tours 1801, 1813, 1818*, ed. D. Alan Stevenson, 1946. Report of the Select Committee on Lighthouses, 1834. Royal Commission on Lights, Buoys and Beacons, 1861.
[22] Personal communication, Jane Wilson, Trinity House, London.
[23] Royal Commission on Lights, Buoys and Beacons, 1861, p.299. For background information *see* L. Lloyd, *The Port of Caernarfon, 1793-1900* (Caernarfon, 1989), chapter 9.

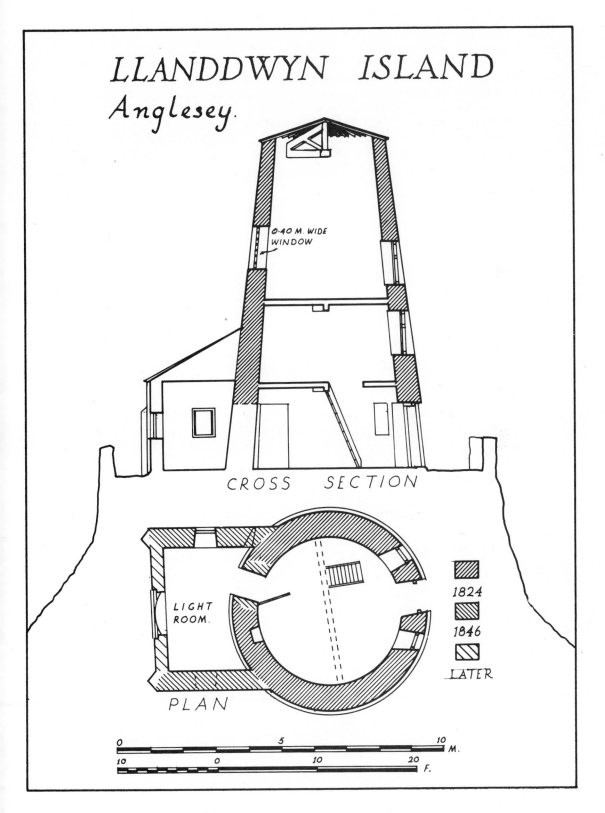

# LLANDDWYN ISLAND
## Anglesey.

0.40 M. WIDE
WINDOW

CROSS SECTION

LIGHT ROOM.

PLAN

1824

1846

LATER

0    5    10 M.

10    0    10    20 F.

A short distance to the south-east is a smaller conical stone tower with a domed top. Presumably this simple structure is earlier than the taller tower. Its precise date is uncertain; both towers are shown on the manuscript 1818-23 Ordnance Survey 2 inches to 1 mile map, but not on Lewis Morris's chart of 1800. The lantern in the base of the lower tower had been discontinued by 1975 and a light was put instead on top of this day-mark. The walls of this structure are about 2.03m (6ft 8ins) in radius and 0.91m (3ft) thick with a door to the north-north-west. Its rubble-built walls show signs of cracking on the west. The thickness of the dome has resulted in the cable leading to the electric light on the roof being fixed to the external wall.

*The cottages at Llanddwyn Island are now used as craft workshops. The two lighthouses on the island may both have originated as unlit markers. The community here also serviced pilot-boats and life boats.*

# Bardsey: Ynys Enlli,
## Gwynedd (Caernarfonshire. SH 111206) ***

*The site is significant for having the tallest square tower of any lighthouse site in the British Isles.*

The 30.2m (99ft) high Bardsey tower of 1821 is a sea light set on the southern tip of Bardsey Island off the Lleyn Peninsula and marks the division between Caernarfon and Cardigan Bays. Application for a light here was first made in 1816 by Lt. Thomas Evans R.N., but several other applications made in 1820 finally resulted in the building of the tower by the Corporation of Trinity House. The light was first exhibited on 24 December 1821.[24] Joseph Nelson is recorded as both engineer and builder, but the heavy weathered string-course near the base and the blocked and hooded directional-light window show the influence of Daniel Alexander, who succeeded Samuel Wyatt as architect to Trinity House, and under whom Nelson served. Joseph Nelson is

*The unusual square tower at Bardsey had a ground-floor oil-store ceiled by a shallow vault. There is a central counter-weight tube for the rotative mechanism.*

---

[24]  Royal Commission on Lights and Buoys, 1861.

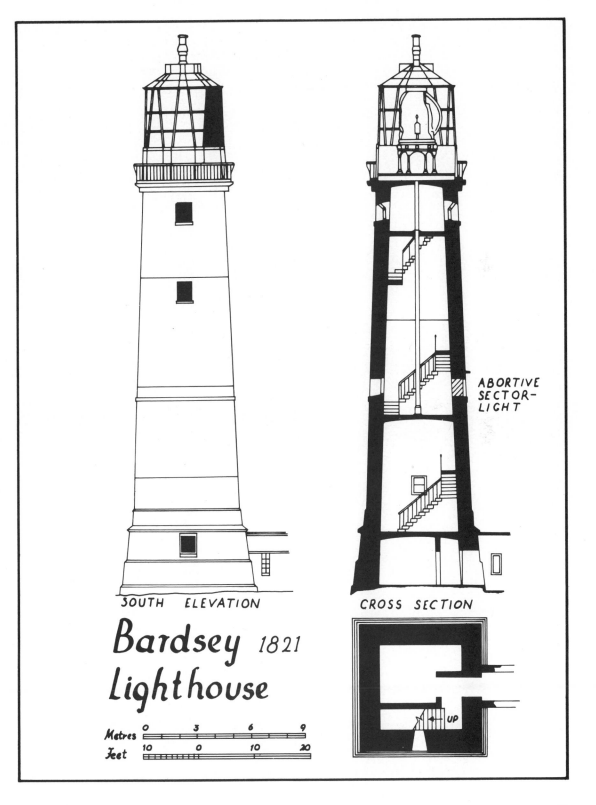

SOUTH ELEVATION

CROSS SECTION

ABORTIVE
SECTOR-
LIGHT

UP

# Bardsey 1821
# Lighthouse

| Metres | 0 | | 3 | | 6 | | 9 |
| Feet | 10 | | 0 | | 10 | | 20 |

*Bardsey Light's gallery railings are bellied out like those of the contemporary Salt Island tower.*

associated with the design of at least fifteen lighthouses, mostly in the Bristol Channel. This handsome tower is well built of ashlar limestone unplastered inside and out, but painted externally with white and red bands; the stone was supplied by William Thomas. It is unusual amongst Trinity House towers of this period in being square in plan. It is also one of the few lighthouses of this authority to retain its original gallery railings. These are of iron and bellied (*i.e.* curved out in width at their crowns) towards the top. Other examples are to be seen in the disused harbour light at Salt Island, Holyhead, designed by John Rennie in the same year, on Rennie's companion tower of 1818 at Howth, and also on the east coast of Britain's Great

or Inner Farne light of 1811, designed by Daniel Alexander with Joseph Nelson recorded as builder. When the present lantern was fitted in 1856 it was found possible to retain the original gallery railings.

The tower has a powerful and elaborately enriched plinth about 4m (13ft) high. At ground level the structure is 7.6m (25ft) square reducing to 6.1m (20ft) at the top of the plinth and to 4.6m (15ft) at the summit of the tower below the crowning cornice which is itself 5.5m (18ft) square. The walls are 1.2m (4ft) thick at their base diminishing to under 0.9m (3ft) at 22m (72ft), above this the lantern makes a total height of 30.2m (99ft). The tower is non-residential, but has a floor over the 2.4m (8ft) high ground-floor oil-store which is ceiled by a shallow

*The exposed position of Bardsey Lighthouse Station, as depicted by Douglas Hague.*

vault of slabs. A similar vault carries the next stage 9.1m (29ft 8ins) above the ground at the level of the blocked low-light; above this the interior is open and contains a cantilevered stair. In the east wall of this second floor can be traced the outline of a 1.2m (4ft) wide blocked window with a shouldered head, and this feature is clearly expressed externally by recessed blocking and a projecting or hooded lintel. Nothing is known of the history of this opening which was clearly intended to display a sector light, perhaps intended to assist landing. As its blocking stones are dressed in exactly the same fashion as the surrounding masonry this may well have been done at the time of construction and the low-light may never have functioned. The external hood closely resembles those at Harwich and Lundy, both designed by Daniel Alexander (1768-1846) in 1818. As Nelson was employed as builder at Lundy, it is tempting to consider that the idea came from there. The original illumination was by reflectors, but these were changed for a dioptric (refracting) apparatus in 1838; the appearance of the original lantern is not known. The present lantern of 1856 is a 4.27m (14ft) wide chamfered octagon, its glazing is rhomboidal with two horizontal glazing bars and inclined uprights. The light itself remained fixed, rather than revolving.[25] The lower iron walling is 1.5m (5ft) high

---

[25]   Ibid.

and the glazed area 3m (10ft) high, its cost was £2,950 16s 7d. As already noted, the original railings were retained as they were just curved enough to enable keepers of average girth to continue to circulate around the new apparatus. The present revolving apparatus was installed in 1873[26] and this entailed the reconstruction of the lantern floor and the provision of a weight tube down to the second floor. This gives a group of five flashes and the vapourizing oil-lamp was replaced by electricity shortly before 1973. The installation of the generators resulted in the fog-signal changing to the electrical emitters installed in a new building to the west.

The original keepers' houses have a connecting corridor to the lighthouse tower through its east wall. They have now been converted to other uses and new dwellings have been erected to the south-east. The station also retains a circular, nineteenth-century vaulted oil store or magazine. Bardsey is also unusual amongst island rock stations in lacking any sort of harbour or quay facilities, although one was planned just before World War II. As it is on a well established migratory route the tower has claimed many bird victims. The Royal Society for the Protection of Birds and Trinity House have attempted to reduce this slaughter. They included the provision of perches on top of the lantern and flood-lighting the tower to lessen the dazzle of the lamp; alas, neither has proved successful.

The Bardsey Lighthouse is now an automatic light operated from the Holyhead Control Centre. The Keepers' houses are leased out to the Bardsey Island Trust.

# St. Tudwal's West Island: Ynys Tudwal, Gwynedd (Caernarfonshire. SH 334252) *

A small, now unmanned, light marking the north end of Cardigan Bay. The stone tower, 10.7m (35 ft) high, was built in 1877. The keepers' cottages are now privately owned and used as a holiday home. The Chance Bros. optic of 1876 was the first occulting apparatus made by the firm.

## West Wales Lights

The Skerries and Smalls lighthouses shielded the outer extremities of the north and south headlands of Wales from the vast flow of eighteenth- and nineteenth-century empire traffic that skirted Wales on the approaches to the thriving British port of Liverpool. However, the inner lights of these headlands were built in response to the petitions of the Welsh mariners carrying lesser volumes of traffic to and from the smaller mid Wales ports of Cardigan Bay. Even so, the dues from this trade were insufficient to light the estuarine ports on a large scale though there was clearly some desire for this to be done. The following mid nineteenth-century summary of the situation was made after the construction of the South Bishop Light (built in response to the requests of Cardigan traders) but before the construction of St. Tudwal's light (in the 1870s), and of Strumble Head Lighthouse (1908-09) in response to the requirements of the new Irish ferry service from Fishguard.

In 1845 William Harries, clerk, J.P. for the County of Pembroke, responded to an enquiry from the clerk of the Parliamentary Lighthouse Committee in the following terms:

'In answer to your inquiry respecting the management of lighthouses on this coast, I beg leave to state that I have had communications with the most influential master mariner's and other persons connected with shipping in this vicinity, and their unanimous opinion is that a great loss of life and property annually takes place for want of some harbour of refuge, and of course, a lighthouse connected with it, on the whole Welsh coast, from St. David's Head to Bardsey Island. Not a single lighthouse exists in all that extent of coast, nor is there at present, a single harbour to which vessels can safely run in all winds, and when suddenly overtaken by storms.

It is the general wish of the seafaring persons in this neighbourhood to bring the subject under the notice of Government, and a meeting had been held and a petition drawn up on the affair before I received your circular.'[27] Despite attempts no large lighthouse structures were completed along the lesser navigation channels of the west coast of Wales.

---

[26]  Trinity House Records.
[27]  The 1845 Parliamentary Report on Lighthouses, Appendix No.65, p.652.

# Ynys y Brawd, Barmouth: Abermo,
## Gwynedd (Merioneth. SH 615152)

Two attempts were made in 1839 and 1843 to build towers on Ynys y Brawd, an island off Barmouth, but both were washed away before completion. A more modern beacon stands at the east end of the island.[28]

Small harbour lights or leading beacons are a feature of all ports. In mid Wales a very recent addition has been the green and white concrete tower added to the early nineteenth-century south pier of Aberystwyth Harbour.

# Strumble Head: Ynys Meicel,
## Dyfed (Pembrokeshire. SM 892413) **

*This building is significant as one of the few early twentieth-century lights in Wales.*

A proposal to erect a lighthouse here had been made in the Trinity House Court Minutes for 7 July 1825 but it came to nothing. The present light was built in 1908-09 and marks Strumble Head, situated to the west of Fishguard Harbour. To some extent the present light replaced the light-vessel previously

moored in the south of Cardigan Bay. The 16.8m (55ft) high tower stands on the summit of a small island, Ynys Meicel, reached by an iron bridge from

---

[28] E.R. Jones, *A History of Barmouth & Vicinity*, 1909, 45-6.

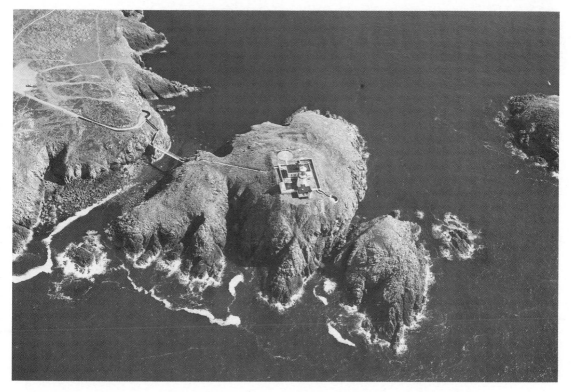

*Strumble Head Light is one of the later lights built to guide vessels safely into the ports of Wales (Dyfed Archaeological Trust).*

*Strumble Head has a large Chance lens.*

the north-east end of Pen Caer promontory, a conspicuous headland 8km (5 miles) north-west of Fishguard.

This circular stone tower tapers from a diameter of 6.6m (21ft 6ins) above its base plinth. Its casement windows with protruding lintels have fine brass fittings inside. A plain string-course at the summit of the tower swells into an ovolo-moulded cornice with a heavy protruding band, and this forms the base of the gallery which has cast-iron railings consisting of three horizontal rails supported by uprights capped with plainly decorated finials. The lantern is original with a 4.14m (13ft 7ins) diameter lower iron wall topped by smallish diamond panes with the blind of the light made up of diamond-shaped iron panels. The whole is crowned by a flat dome with a vent and weathervane. The lantern contains a fine large Chance lens floating in a mercury bath. The illumination was changed from paraffin to electricity in 1949. A slate plaque in the lantern-room is inscribed with a verse from Psalm 127:

> ' Except the Lord Build the house.
> They labour in vain that build it
> Except the Lord keep the city
> The Watchman maketh but in vain '

There is a water tank with a slate cover under the lantern-room. The stairs up the tower surround a large circular well. Paraffin to fuel the light was pumped upwards by a handle from a tank in the base of the tower which was filled from the mainland using an inverted syphon or 'U-tube'. A novel feature was that one handrail of the bridge and steps giving access to the island was actually part of the iron U-pipe conveying fuel from a tank in the mainland to one at the same level on the island, parts of this apparatus still survive.

An electronic tannoy fog-signal was installed in 1969. A 'Blondin' cableway carries stores from the mainland. Below the lighthouse is a flagpole protected by a circular wall, diameter 5.6m (18ft 2ins). Today the tower is reached by an 24m (80ft) long aluminium bridge, replacing the original iron bridge in 1963.

Strumble Head is now an automatic light controlled from St. Ann's Head but regularly visited by an attendant.

*The bridge handrail was a paraffin supply pipe.*

# South Bishop: Em-Sger,
## Dyfed (Pembrokeshire. SM 651226) ***

*This building is noteworthy for having the earliest completely unaltered lantern in a working lighthouse in England and Wales and is a good example of James Walker's well-planned Welsh lights.*

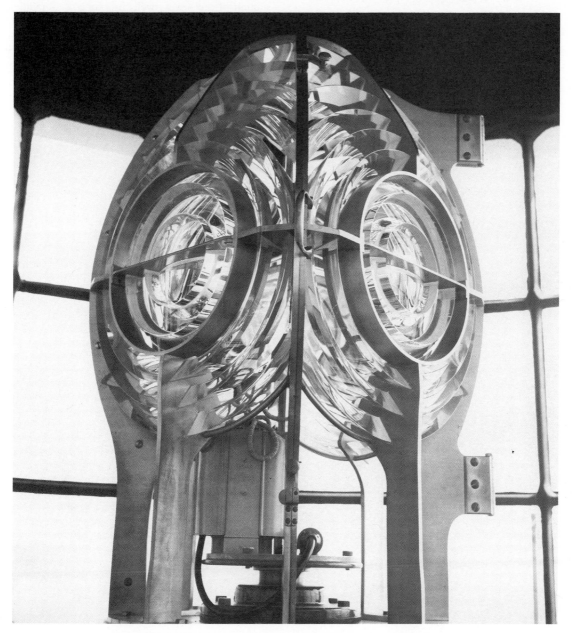

*The early lantern at the South Bishop light now houses a Stone Chance optic of the early 1970s. Fresnel lenses are surrounded by concentric circles of glass prisms to direct the light-rays out to sea.*

*South Bishop had two landing-places leading up to the dwelling-houses connected to the lighthouse.*

It is set on one of the larger and the most southerly of a villainous scatter of islets and rocks lying 4.8km (3 miles) to the west of Ramsey Island, about 8km (5 miles) south-west of St David's Head. An application to build a light was first made in 1831 by the traders of Cardigan, but it was not successful until June 1834. The tower occupies the summit of a barren lava rock about 244m (800ft) by 122m (400ft) and 30.5m (100ft) high; the landing-place is situated a little south of the north-east corner. This attractive lighthouse came into operation in 1839 and was, unfortunately, converted into unmanned station in the 1970s. The 11.3m (37ft) high tower was designed by James Walker but is unlike his other buildings; the superintendent of works was W.D. Frazer with George Burrell assisting. The circular tower is built of granite as are the contemporary dwellings. It is a very slightly tapering tower capped by a rather feeble corbelled cornice, which has most unusual locally-made iron railings instead of carrying his usual battlemented parapet. The profile of the railings is bellied out in early nineteenth-century style, but the single intermediate horizontal rail has a mean, modern appearance. The fine original iron lantern dated 1838 is a rare survival and bears the inscription:

'WILKINSON, LONG ACRE LONDON 1838'.

It is the oldest completely unaltered lantern in a working lighthouse in England and Wales. It is 4.28m (14ft) in diameter, the glazed part is 3.05m (10ft) high and retains its original conical roof with ball-finial vent. The glazing is of panes 0.74m (2ft 5ins) high by 0.53m (1ft 9ins) wide and consists of four rows of 24 panes. The upper and lower rows are of flat glass, but the middle two rows have been replaced by curved panes to eliminate false flashes, a minor modification made by the early 1970s when the present Stone Chance lens was fitted. The lantern is carried on a 1.37m (4ft 6ins) iron lower wall which retains the original brass vent covers; the base of the iron lower wall coincides with the level of the outer gallery which is unusual in being 1.07m (3ft 6ins) above the floor level of the service-room.

*The Wilkinson lantern of 1838 at South Bishop is the oldest unaltered lantern in England and Wales.*

This floor is carried on four original cast-iron beams; the inner gallery has now been extended over the whole lantern, but the outer ring is carried on brackets which although shaped appear to be of steel, and may have replaced the original cast-iron fittings. The service-room was strengthened with rolled-steel joists when a revolving apparatus was fitted together with a central weight tube extending the full height of the tower. The original Argand lamps were removed in 1858 when the optic from Lundy was installed, although it was reported in 1861 that only the eight central lenses were in use without upper and lower refractive prisms. This reduced arrangement was lit by a four-burner lamp. The cast-iron beams used to carry both the service-room and the floor over the oil-store or cellar are 0.23m (9ins) deep with upper flanges 0.15m (6ins) wide and the lower of 0.1m (4in). The tower is not residential and contains a stone geometric stair, the interior is lit by one round-headed window containing its original sashes. The tower is entered from a wide corridor connecting it with the dwellings at a mezzanine level, from this one stair leads down to the oil-store and the other up to the base of the main stair. The entrance into the tower is a wide opening beneath a Tudor-style arch; the form of this arch is repeated, although plainer, at the dwelling end of the corridor. The two original houses are symmetrically planned. Modern windows have been fitted to the south-east front but the old sashes survive on the north. Although more modest than the grandiose layout of the Skerries, the station is carefully planned with extra buildings added within the walled enclosure on the north-west to house compressors and other equipment. The older whitewashed range has a hipped roof and the more modern a flat roof. A helicopter landing-pad has recently been provided to the south-west of the tower. When visited by the commissioners during the preparation of the report of 1861, the keepers were complimented on the careful way in which they washed out the salt from the water channels before filling the rock-cut tanks with drinking water. There are two landing-places on the west and east; the latter only is now used. The paths and steps are lined with massive iron hand-rail posts which, with several other fittings, are described in the field- and letter-books of George Burrell (the superintendent of works) which have been acquired by the National Library of Wales.

The South Bishop Lighthouse was automated in 1983 and is controlled from St Ann's Head.

# Skokholm, Dyfed (Pembrokeshire. SM729046) **

*Interesting as the last lighthouse tower to be built of traditional materials in Britain.*

It lies on the south-west end of Skokholm Island and was first lit in 1915-16. Its red (warning) light is five miles west-north-west of St Ann's Head. The 17.7m

*Skokholm was the last British stone-built light.*

(58ft) high octagonal tower was the last tower of traditional construction to be erected by Trinity House. Its design, with the lower part of the tower incorporated into flat-roofed two-storeyed dwellings with a symmetrical entrance front, is reminiscent of several Scottish sites, including May and Inchkeith. The presence of the structure of the tower within the dwellings is expressed externally by a slight vertical projection and further emphasized by a square porch. Above the flat roof of the two-storeyed dwellings the square structure of the tower slopes into the shape of an octagon. The diameter of the lantern is 3.45m (11ft 4ins) with normal diagonal panes and iron glazing bars. The fog-signal engine-house occupies the seaward side of the dwellings and the typhoon-horns are situated at the angles.

A plaque inside the tower records that it was officially opened in 1915. The buildings are said to have been built of stone rubble but all is now rendered and painted white. A new Stone Chance Optic, lit and operated electrically, had been fitted by the early 1970s.

The Skokholm Lighthouse is now automatically operated and controlled from St. Ann's Head.

# The Smalls: Gwales
## Dyfed (Pembrokeshire. SM 467089) ****

*This is a site of international importance and is noteworthy as the tallest and most graceful Welsh lighthouse. It was built on an exposed rock and is the finest work by the prolific engineer, James Walker. The archaeological*

*remains on the Smalls Rock of the first piled-light to be built in Britain, and perhaps in the world, are of considerable significance. This was also the site of the first attempt to use iron in the construction of a lighthouse (and possibly the first constructional use of cast-iron in the modern world).*

Geographically the Smalls reef is the most westerly point of Wales, a reef of rocks 27km (17 miles) off the Pembrokeshire coast. Built a few feet above high-water level, the tower is 42m (138ft) high and tapers gracefully from a stepped base. Its solid base has shallow steps to the level of the entrance 7.6m (25 ft) above the rock. The elevated entrance itself is reached by a bronze ladder built in the wall of the tower. The first stone was laid in 1858 and the tower was completed in 1861. The original lantern survives. In 1932 it was capped by a structure carrying a wind-generator for radio communications; strangely, this was not satisfactory and it was removed. In 1978 the whole lantern was strengthened, and a helicopter landing-deck fitted to its top. During this modernization programme the vaporizing oil-lamps and the subsidiary red sector-light were replaced, and the electrical generator, needed for the light and electronic fog-signals, was fitted within the tower;

this involved the removal of some of the comfortable mural steps and their replacement by vertical ladders.

Walker appears to have been the first engineer to consider lighthouse sanitation. As already noted, his Needles (Isle of Wight), Wolf Rock and Smalls lighthouses were amongst those to contain water-closets, although it is said that waves caused an embarrassing upsurge.

Apart from these alterations, nothing has been done to the structure of the tower and the masonry is in impeccable condition, the joints being as tight and impenetrable as the day they were laid and good for another century or more.

The remarkable original light at the Smalls, as with many others, was built as a result of pressure from the ranks of merchants, shipowners and seamen. For ships sailing south through the Irish Sea, the Smalls and the adjacent Hats and Barrels,

*James Walker's graceful tower of 1858-61 stands on the exposed sea-girt rock of the Smalls.*

*What was probably the world's earliest piled-light was located on the highest point of the Smalls Rock, and continued standing whilst the more substantial tower alongside was built in 1858-61.*
*(By permission of the National Library of Wales).*

along with the vicious tidal rips, were a deadly threat and claimed many wrecks. Early in the 1770s suggestions were made that the Smalls Rock should be lit and finally, in 1773, a Quaker, John Phillips, Master of St. George's Dock, Liverpool, obtained a lease of the Rock.

Little is known about Phillips himself or what prompted Henry Whiteside, a musical-instrument maker, to have made a model for a proposed light on the Skerries. Phillips was already agent for the Skerries light, an orthodox stone tower capped by a coal fire, but wanted his light to be 'so singular a construction as to be known from all others in the world' and commissioned Whiteside to construct a novel pile-built structure.[29]

The unique structure designed by Whiteside was demolished in 1861, when the present magnificent tower was commissioned, but a careful survey of the remains which existed until the construction of a helicopter-pad on the surface of the rock, together with a study of early sketches, drawings and accounts, has made it possible to produce a drawing of the lighthouse as it must have appeared in the mid nineteenth century.

We do not know to what extent Whiteside's choice of design was influenced by the need to economize, although it is known Phillips was near bankruptcy. However, rather than build a massive masonry tower to defy the elements, he adopted the ingenious plan of a piled structure through which the

*Prior to the building of the Smalls helicopter landing-pad in 1972 it was possible to record the surviving post-holes and stubs of the important early towers.*

---

[29]   Much of the material on the early Smalls Lighthouse is drawn from E. Freeman, *The Solva Saga* (Llanblethian, 1958).

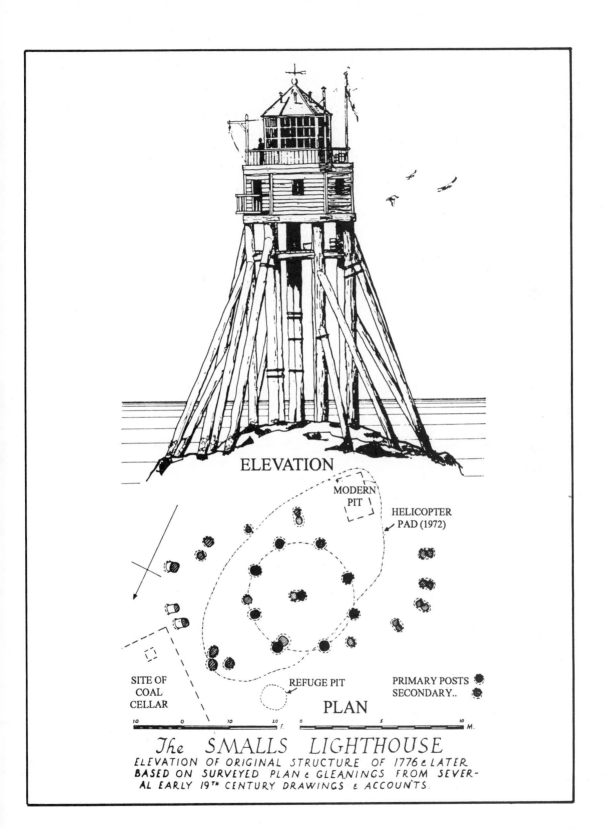

ELEVATION

MODERN PIT

HELICOPTER PAD (1972)

SITE OF COAL CELLAR

REFUGE PIT

PRIMARY POSTS

SECONDARY..

PLAN

The SMALLS LIGHTHOUSE
ELEVATION OF ORIGINAL STRUCTURE OF 1776 & LATER
BASED ON SURVEYED PLAN & GLEANINGS FROM SEVER-
AL EARLY 19TH CENTURY DRAWINGS & ACCOUNTS.

fury of the seas could pass freely. The fact that Whiteside's somewhat bucolic structure of rough-hewn oak posts stood from 1776 to 1861 is the best possible vindication of his skill and judgement.

At first he planned to use an open framework of three sectional cast-iron stanchions (0.305m - 12in in diameter) surrounded by a number of pillars of wood. Presumably the cast-iron pipework, and timbers, of the pillars were of the same order of magnitude as the 12.8m (42ft) posts later used. The prefabricated structure was set up in a field (Y Gamlyn) at the end of Solva Harbour and was then erected on the Smalls Rock during 1775. However this composite structure was abandoned without a light in the winter of 1775 when it was found that the wooden and iron posts would not work in unison, and that the iron ones were working loose in the rock. The wooden pillars could flex during storms while the iron pillars remained rigid except for their opening joints. Whiteside decided that the iron supports were too brittle, and it also proved to impossible to secure flanged joints as the iron bolts connecting the sections of iron tubing worked loose; part of one of the cast-iron stanchions was later to be seen in use as a bollard on the quay at Solva, the delightful sheltered haven on the north side of St. Bride's Bay, which Whiteside used as his base.

The 37km (23 mile) voyage from Solva to the rock must have taken a considerable time and often have ended in failure to make a landing because of an increase or change in the wind. Those who have never landed on the rock can have little conception of the prodigious difficulties facing lighthouse engineers; a landing cannot be made at will. Even in summer there are many days when landings on two consecutive days are rare, while the landing of equipment and stones weighing over a tonne demands patience, courage and ingenuity. The erection of a building on such an impossible site, especially in the days before steam power, cannot fail to excite the admiration of even the most unromantic. Conversely, on calm days when landing was possible, vessels often could not move for want of wind.

Whiteside's first task for the reconstruction of the lighthouse in timber was to mark out a circle 6.5m in diameter, and to cut holes for eight posts about 0.75m across, with a ninth central post. The necessary post-holes had to be cut in the exposed surface of the rock; the work was done under conditions of great difficulty. All were about 14m (46ft) in length and secured to the rock by a grouting of molten lead

*Some weathered stubs of the 1776 Smalls Lighthouse survive together with eleven post-holes.*

in deeply drilled holes so that the posts stood some 12.8m (42ft) above the surface of the rock. The overall height of the lighthouse was 19.8m (65ft) and it was 6.7m (22ft) in diameter. On top, and reached by a rope ladder, was the keepers' accommodation and above that was the lantern displaying the fixed lamps. They were octagonal in plan with a raised walk around the lantern, which was fitted with iron railings 'in order that the windows might be kept clean.' The new light was operational by January 1777. The piled design enabled the waves to wash through freely and it was the forerunner of all pile-lights of the nineteenth century. There are vivid descriptions of terrifying storm conditions when waves lashed the bottom of the cabin. Each pillar was originally braced on its eastern side, but during the existence of the light it was found necessary to add stiffening raking struts on its western side also and to double up or to replace existing ones, the final number being 31. As already noted, the construction of a helicopter-pad on the rock surface

*The original Smalls lantern has been modified.*

in 1972 has obliterated most of the principal post-stubs or post-holes. However, the weathered stubs of two original posts survive, together with eleven post-holes for the raking struts, some with their lower posts, of which a number are paired.

The fitting of new fuel- and water-tanks at about the same time has destroyed the original small rock-cut coal cellar, but a refuge for tools is still visible. These original rock-cut stores were necessitated by the meagre space available in the super-structure of a pile-top construction like the first Smalls light.

The original Smalls Lighthouse was a brave achievement although it did not impress some contemporaries by its use of relatively humble materials. Robert Stevenson, the founder of the great dynasty of Scottish lighthouse engineers, is said to have commented after a visit to the Smalls in 1801 that the building had 'no better appellation than a raft of timber rudely put together; the material ill-suited for a permanent structure.'

Nevertheless the lighthouse proved to be a successful building. It can claim a unique position in the history of lighthouse economics as it was almost certainly the most profitable lighthouse in the world. Even after the Act of 1836, when it was administered by Trinity House, who had greatly reduced the dues, it was still bringing in an income of £22,000 a year, against which was set the annual rent of £5 to the Crown for the rocks, the modest wages of the keepers, and the cost of the fuel.

By the time of the takeover in 1836, the lighthouse had passed to Phillips's grandson, the Rev. A.B. Buchanan, who displayed an astute understanding of temporal affairs. In 1823 he had refused an offer of £148,430, considering it inadequate, and finally, with 41 years of his lease to run, he was compensated with the considerable sum of £170,468. The Smalls, like the Skerries, can also claim a remarkable place in the annals of economic history. Even in 1852, after Trinity House had lowered the dues, its annual income was still £22,759.[30]

The Smalls tower now carries an automatic light which is controlled from St. Ann's Head.

[30] Other sources used in this account are: I. Emlyn (J. Williams), *The Smalls: a sketch of the old lighthouse* (Solva, 1858); E.C. Woods and J.S. Rees, 'The Smalls Lighthouse', *Transactions of the Lancashire and Cheshire Historical Society* (1948); Report of the Royal Commission on Lights and Buoys, 1861; T. Williams, *Life of Sir James Douglass* (1900), and an article by Douglas Hague in *Country Life* for 28.2.1963.

# St. Ann's Head, Dyfed (Pembrokeshire. SM 806028) **

*This location is important as the probable site of a medieval lighthouse, the first built in Wales. Towers of 1800 and 1844 remain standing above the ground.*

There is every reason to believe that St Ann's Head, covering and marking the entrance to the great harbour of Milford Haven, is the site of the earliest lighthouse in Wales. Until recent years the potentialities of this great harbour had never been fully exploited, but in medieval times it was a port of departure for Ireland. For about one hundred years following the Napoleonic period, and for one hundred and fifty years before the present vast oil-terminals were built, it had been a busy naval base centred around Pembroke Dock. The Dale peninsula, terminating in St. Ann's Head and protecting the great harbour from the west, made the harbour entrance difficult to identify from the sea.

The greatest historical event at the Haven was the landing of Henry Tudor on his way to Bosworth Field in 1485 and there is a reasonable tradition that after he was crowned he erected a chapel to commemorate the landing. This may have been the now disappeared chapel of St Ann's. George Owen in the late sixteenth century, giving details of making a landfall, stressed the importance of the tower of St Ann's Chapel as a landmark.[31] He described the chapel as being 'decayed' with a round tower about 20ft (6.1m) high resembling a windmill or pigeon-house, but he makes no mention of a light.

The first reference to a light occurs in 1662 when Trinity House was granted permission to erect a light;[32] no details were given, but it seems most likely that use was made of the existing tower. Two Dutch charts published in 1663 by Gerard and Johannes van Keulan show one light on the small-

---

[31]  G. Owen, *The Description of Penbrokshire*, ed. H. Owen, Vol.II., p. 551.
[32]  Trinity House Court Minutes, 1661-65.

*The circular compressor house at St Ann's Head with dwellings, the 1844 low light and new fog-horn beyond. This view is taken from the high light of 1800 which was operated together with the 1844 tower until 1910.*

scale chart, but two lights are shown on their larger-scale chart, and one of these labelled 'Old Light Tower'. Captain Grenville Collins in his *Coasting Pilot* of 1693 includes two similar charts, but in this case the larger-scale version only marks one tower. Tantalizingly, John Whormby, a senior clerk of Trinity House, wrote a history of the Corporation in 1746 (published in 1861) and promised to deal with the station in detail but never did.[33] The first satisfactory evidence of a structure built and used as a lighthouse is in 1713 when, in answer to a petition, Joseph Allen, the local landowner at Dale, was granted a ninety-nine year lease to erect a lighthouse and to levy dues, providing that 'out of the profits thereof' he should pay what 'he thought reasonable towards the relief of the poor depending on the Corporation'.[34] Mention is made then of only one tower, although later in the century there were two. It is possible that these were the medieval tower and that the second was a new construction, later to become the high light. It would appear that the two coal lights were a success, both in marking the entrance from the west and, perhaps more importantly, in giving a safe lead in from the south.

When the two towers were in line, ships would be sure of passing to the west of the Crow and Toe Rocks which lie about a mile off Linney Head, six miles to the south-south-east. However towards the end of the eighteenth century they were said to have become unsatisfactory, and Captain Huddart was called in to survey the site and make recommendations. In 1798 John H. Allen made an application for an advance of £500 on account of the £2000 which Trinity House had agreed to make available.[35] In May 1800 it was reported that the alterations and improvements had been completed.[36] Three months later Mr. Allen reported that the works had cost £600 more than the estimated sum, and that this was due not only to the 'great advances in the prices of labour and materials' but also because it had been found necessary to take down and rebuild both towers instead of one.[37]

---

[33]   Whormby, J, *An Account of the Corporation of Trinity House of Deptford Strond...* (1746; London, 1861).
[34]   Trinity House Court Minutes, 21 May 1713.
[35]   Ibid., 6 December 1798.
[36]   Ibid., 1 May 1800.

*The low light at St Ann's now forms part of one of only two manned lighthouse stations in Wales.*

*Modern fog-horn at St Ann's with the 1844 low light and dwellings beyond.*

Captain Huddart went to inspect the work in the same year and was in general satisfied. However the south lighthouse was placed somewhat to the eastward of the site he had recommended, but as this could not lead ships nearer to any danger than some 510m (560yds) when the lights were lined up by shipping, he thought that it was not material.[38] It seems clear that Mr. Allen did not complete the work of demolition. After an inspection of the site in 1813 it was reported that the two old lighthouses were still standing and, as there were so many objects on the point liable to cause confusion in hazy weather, it was recommended that they should be taken down and the old cinder heaps levelled.[39] Details of the lights, their elevation and their distance apart (186m or 203 yds) are given in the *The New Seaman's Guide and Coaster's Companion* of 1821, yet there appears to be no surviving explanation as to why it was found necessary to rebuild the low light in 1844 and to take down the old tower.[40] The 1844 tower is the single one now in use, and despite Huddart's reservations on the siting of the earlier tower, this later one was set even further to the east. At present its red sector covers the Crow

and Toe Rocks, but it must have been used in conjunction with the high light of 1800 which remained in use until 1909. Two towers remain standing, the disused high light of 1800 and the present low light of 1844.

Locating the sites of the earlier towers presents considerable archaeological problems. Some light on the siting and appearance of the earlier towers is to be gleaned from drawings and water-colours made by John (Warwick) Smith, late in the 1790s, and by Charles Norris of Tenby who was painting early in the nineteenth century. These show both earlier towers had coal braziers. A pair of drawings by each artist has been redrawn to an approximately uniform scale and reproduced in the adjoining block of four drawings; they are designed to be consulted in conjunction with the site plan on which each site is named. Smith's sketch no.1 is looking towards Linney Head, and should be compared with sketch

---

[37]  Ibid., 7 August 1800.
[38]  Ibid., 26 June 1800.
[39]  Ibid., 6 May 1813.
[40]  Ibid., 7 May 1844.

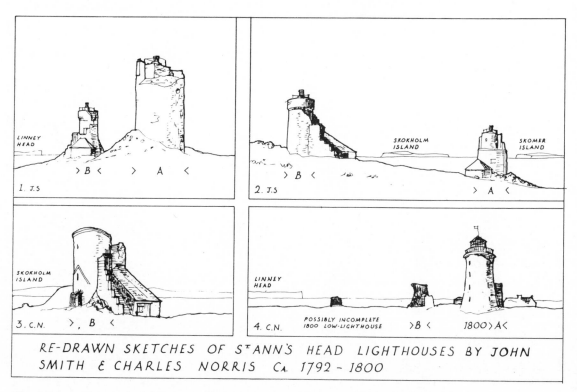

RE-DRAWN SKETCHES OF ST ANN'S HEAD LIGHTHOUSES BY JOHN SMITH & CHARLES NORRIS CA. 1792 - 1800

*The drawings of the early lighthouses at St Ann's present evidence on their former locations.*

no.4 made by Norris some time before 1813. Smith's sketch no.2 is looking the opposite way, with Skokholm Island showing between the two lighthouses; Smith's drawing is a little inaccurate as tower 'B' is shown to be higher than 'A'. This sketch may well have been completed in the studio whilst Smith's sketch no.1 appears to have been drawn in the field. Smith's drawing no.2 should be compared with Norris's sketch no.3 where tower 'B' is shown in more detail. Features like the roof creasing and door, were either not observed by Smith or are lost under a wash. Norris's drawing no.3 is only known from a reproduction, but the observation of the creasing for the roof of a destroyed building, such as a chapel, suggests an arrangement similar to that at Chale Down on the Isle of Wight where a hexagonal lighthouse of *c.*1813 still stands. Norris's sketch no.4. is not a crisp drawing and it is by no means clear what the rather indefinite stump to the left (south) of tower 'B' is; at this time the low light associated with the 1800 high light should have been in equally good condition.

The existence of a large building, apparently with an enclosed courtyard, near 'B' and the present compressor-house, is only recorded on the tithe map of 1847. No trace of it is to be seen on the first

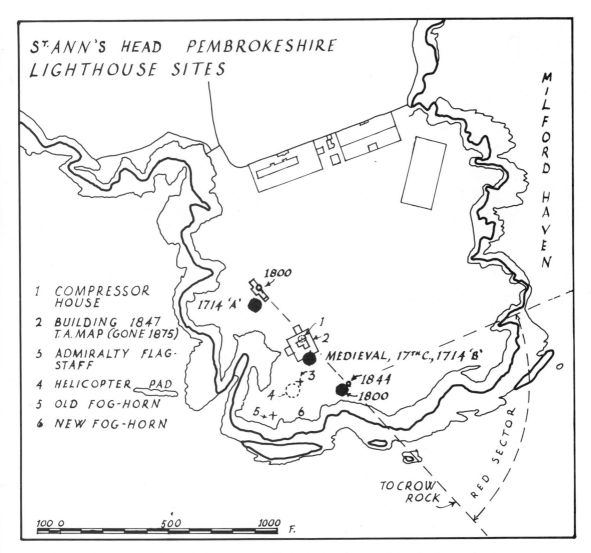

*Map showing the present and vanished structures at St Ann's; based on surviving drawings and maps.*

large-scale (1:2,500) Ordnance Survey map of 1875. During excavations for a helicopter-pad ('4' on the site plan) a crescent of masonry was observed which had every appearance of a lighthouse base. In the centre was a large block of stone forming the seating for a flag-pole, at first it was thought possible that this had been sited in the middle of an earlier destroyed tower, but it was found that the wall was not a full circle. The curved and battered wall was in fact a screen to an Admiralty flag-staff. More recently the old fog-horn has been replaced by an electrically operated one, '6' on the plan. Available air photographs do not help in the interpretation of this complicated site where all the unwanted buildings have been most carefully and thoroughly erased.

The old light of 1800, which is 19.8m (65ft) high, remained in use until 1910,[41] and is now crowned by a barbarous concrete observation box. In 1861 its height was recorded as 22.9m (75ft),[42] but this must have been an error as it could never have been more than 19.8m (65ft) to the top of the lantern. A sunk panel above the entrance is now blank, but is said to have born the date 1800. The lighthouse in use now was built in 1844 and is a squat octagonal 12.8m (42ft) high building with a red sector-light covering Crow and Toe Rocks; it apparently replaced another of 1800 which was incorrectly sited too far eastward. The keepers' houses built with the 1844 lighthouse have been replaced by the present range of dwellings to the north-east.

In 1967 a new low light was placed in the sea between the two navigation channels (on the site of the Mid Channel Rocks) to the south of the headland to assist the entrance of larger tankers, and an ambitious scheme of underwater blasting was undertaken to facilitate the portage of giant tankers (VLCC's). In view of the deliberate policy of levelling structures in the nineteenth century, and with military works in the last two wars, the possibility of recovering the plans of the medieval establishment is remote. However, recent aerial photographs taken by the Dyfed Archaeological

*The upper picture shows the old fog-horn at St Ann's and below is the high light of 1800, now crowned by a concrete observation box.*

---

[41] Personal communication, Jane Wilson, Trinity House, London.
[42] Royal Commission Report on Lights, Buoys & Beacons, 1861, p.101.

Trust do show the trace of a building aligned east-west on the headland.[43]

St. Ann's is one of only two old lighthouses in Wales that remain as manned stations, serving as a control point for the remote surrounding lights at Skokholm and South Bishop Islands, the Smalls Rock, Strumble Head and on the automatic St. Govan's Lightship.[44]

# Milford Haven: Aberdaugleddyf, Dyfed (Pembrokeshire).

Apart from the early lights at St Ann's Head marking the entrance of the haven, it was not until 1870 that any internal lighthouses were built within the vast harbour. Then two leading light 'beacons' in low, square, stone towers were erected at Great Castle Head, about four miles west of Milford, in order to safely guide ships into the harbour.

# Front (Lit) Beacon or Mark, Great Castle Head, Milford Haven (SM 847060) *

James Douglass, engineer-in-chief of Trinity House, designed the twin leading sea marks on Great Castle Head. The front (light) beacon or mark stands on the cliff edge of the south-western side of Great Castle Head (which is itself on the north shore of Milford Haven). This consists of a square, stone tower some 5.18m (17ft) high and 3.96m (13ft) wide with dwellings alongside. The 0.48m (1ft 7ins) wide walls stand on a plinth 0.58m (1ft 11ins) high and are topped by two plain bands of masonry which form a cornice 0.61m (2ft) from the summit of the tower. The entrance door is on the north-western side.

A light-window 0.46m (1ft 6ins) wide faces the south-west. Since about 1958 a sector-light has been shown from a lantern fixed to the roof of the building, as well as from the light-window. In 1970 the light was changed to a sealed beam shown from the roof, to lead with a new light from Little Castle Head (SM 852 066).

# Rear (Lit) Beacon or Mark, Great Castle Head, Milford Haven (SM 848061) *

This beacon is situated 159m (174yds) to the north-east of the Front Light at Great Castle Head, and when the two are in line they lead through the west channel between St. Ann's Head and the Mid Channel Rocks.

The structure of this mark has been reduced from its original height of 12.8m (42ft) down to its halfway stage so as not to obscure the new mark on Little Castle Head. It had a similar cornice to the front mark and stands on the earthen rampart of an Iron Age promontory fort. On the south-eastern elevation were two windows and a doorway, with the arms of Trinity House displayed on a terracotta plaque below the upper window. Both marks were later transferred to the Milford Haven Conservancy Board.

The light was shown from the 0.76m (2ft 6ins) square upper window and discontinued in 1970 so as not to obscure the new lit mark on Little Castle Head.

In the 1970s the use of the Front Light at Great Castle Head was supplemented by modern sealed-beam units at West Block House Point, Watwick Point and Little Castle Head, which display the fine quality and functional beauty of reinforced concrete. These utilitarian structures were designed by Posford Pavry Partners, consulting engineers to the Milford Haven Conservancy Board. Navigation lights and other equipment were supplied by A.G.A. (U.K.) Ltd. There are other navigation and warning lights ('leading light beacons') and jetty marks and lights dispersed around the Haven.

[43]  Verbal information, Terry James.
[44]  Personal communication, Trinity House depot, Swansea.

# Watwick Point, Milford Haven: Aberdaugleddyf,
## Dyfed (Pembrokeshire. SM 821044)

A lit beacon designed to lead ships in conjunction with the West Block House Point Light. It is situated about half a mile north-north-east of West Block House Point and the light shines out at a height of 48.5m (159ft). The tower is similar to Little Castle Head, but a good deal taller.

# West Block House Point, Milford Haven: Aberdaugleddyf,
## Dyfed (Pembrokeshire. SM 817036) & a single beacon at SM 818035.

Three beacons are situated on the promontory to the west side of the Milford Haven entrance about a mile north-east of St. Ann's Head. They consist of three octagonal reinforced-concrete towers 9.14m (30ft), 11.28m (37ft) and 14m (46ft) in height, with sides 1ft 6ins in width, surmounted by cantilevered octagonal concrete platforms on which stand sealed-beam lights. Access is by ladders extending up the columns through an opening in the platform. Each column carries a steel day-mark painted black and white.

There is also a beacon light on the cliff below West Block House Fort set up by Trinity House engineers in 1957. This has a second-hand round metal lantern (ex Rame Head) 0.5m (2ft 7ins) in diameter, supported on a bolted iron pedestal, standing on a concrete platform cantilevered from the cliffs and reached by a steeply descending flight of steps.

Other leading-light beacons are situated near Pembroke Dock, Newton and Bullwell in order to lead ships up the Haven as far as Pembroke Dock.

# Caldy: Ynys Bŷr, Dyfed (Pembrokeshire. SS 143959)

A small installation on the south end of Caldy Island off Tenby, erected by Trinity House by 26 January 1829 at a cost of £4,460.[45] It was intended to help coastal traffic, there being a considerable trade in limestone and coal to the more acid regions of central and north Wales. In August 1830 vessels in the limestone trade were allowed to commute the charge made of 1d per ton each time the light was passed into an annual payment of £1, 15s. or 10s. according to their tonnage.[46] However, it was also clearly important to have identifiable lights near the entrance to the Bristol Channel to confirm to long-distance shipping, including vessels engaged in the north American trade, that they were not entering the English Channel. Indeed it can be speculated that the adjoining monastic site may have maintained a light to guide medieval vessels engaged in the Irish, French and coastal trades.

The Caldy Lighthouse is a small, round, brick-lined limestone tower of 17.07m (56 ft), with walls 0.91m (3ft) thick at the base and 2ft 6in at the top. The light is 64m (210ft) above high-water mark and the structure is flanked by keepers' cottages. An application to build the light was made in March 1827 on behalf of traders in Carmarthen Bay. It was engineered and built by Joseph Nelson and first lit in 1829. There is an excellent wash-drawing of the tower under construction by Charles Norris in Cardiff Public Library. The present lantern was fitted around the middle of the last century. In this building Nelson projected his window lintels to balance the sills, as he did on the Longstone of 1826. The light consisted of 20 Argand lamps and reflectors when built but the present helical lantern was fitted later in the nineteenth century.

The flanking two-storey cottages have a one-

---

[45] Report of the Select Committee on Lighthouses, 1834, Appendix 25
[46] Ibid., Appendix 21.

storey linking corridor forming a 'U'-shaped plan with the lighthouse at the centre of the south side. The hipped-roofed and limewashed cottages have coupled octagonal chimneys and there are enclosed gardens to the north.

There is still a lighthouse attendant based on Caldy Island although the cottages are now occupied by private lessees.

# Saundersfoot, Dyfed (Pembrokeshire. SN 138047) *

A modest but typically idiosyncratic light on the end of the south pier of the small coal- and lime-exporting harbour. Built in 1848, it is a quaint square structure with a domed top with the door on the north side. The light is now a modern polycarbonate optic fixed to the top of the dome, but this replaced a very unusual lantern with iron glazing bars supporting an ogee-shaped stone head 0.61m (2ft) in diameter and 0.28m (11ins) high. In 1861 It was illuminated by candles but this was considered inadequate. There was an ingeniously devised tidal light - a float in the harbour was connected by wires

*The small pierhead light at Saundersfoot had a float connected by wires to a red masking glass.*

to a red glass which masked the light when entrance was impossible. The use of the light was discontinued in 1947, with the closure of the local mines but reinstated in 1954 when the port was revived as a yachting harbour.

The tower is constructed of local stone rubble, about 3.05m (10ft) high and 2.18m (7ft 2ins) square, standing on a stone plinth. The unlit interior has a domed roof which consists of large slabs of ashlar and was presumably constructed as a corbelled vault. The old lantern survived in use until about 1930, and was still in the possession of the harbourmaster at the time of a visit in 1971. It was 0.61m (2ft) in diameter enclosing an oil light, and was divided into eight panes, 0.2m (8ins) across and 0.56m (22ins) high, with a vent hole and was bolted to the top of the dome.

The old light had a recorded elevation above the sea of some 4.6m (15ft) and the new light has a height of 6.4m (21ft).

# Burry Port, Dyfed (Carmarthen. SN 444000) *

*Sketch of the disused harbour light on the west pier at Burry Port.*

Now disused, an attractive little harbour light with reflector on the west pier, built in 1842. Erected by permission of Trinity House, and maintained at the joint expense of the proprietors of Burry Port Harbour and the Commissioners of the Burry Navigation. The annual costs were as follows:

| 1842 | £28.10s. |
| 1843 | £32.10s. |
| 1844 | £32.00s. |

As this was a harbour light no direct charge was made to shipping. However, the superintendent of Burry Port Harbour reported in 1845 that buoyage dues not exceeding 1d a ton had been regularly charged since the passing of an Act for the 'Improvement of the Navigation of the Rivers Bury, Loughor and Lliedi' on the 2 July 1813.[47]

The neighbouring small port of Pembrey Old Harbour also had a lighthouse to guide ships into port (SN 436999).[48]

---

[47] Act 53 Geo. 3, cap. 183, cited in the Select Committee Report on Lighthouses of 1845, Appendix 65, p.633.
[48] S. Nicholson, 'Pembrey and Burry Port: their Harbours and Docks', in *Sir Gâr* ed. H. James (Carmarthen, 1991), 121-141.

# Whitford Point: Chwitffordd,
## West Glamorgan (Glamorgan. SS 443973) ***

*Important as the only wave-swept cast-iron tower of large size left in Britain. It may also be the only building from the former copper-producing centre of the world to retain parts of its early copper-sheeted roof and non-ferrous glazing bars.*

An unusual and handsome cast-iron tower built in 1865 to mark the shoals of Whitford Point in the Burry Estuary, replacing an earlier piled structure of 1854 of which there are no remains. The 13.41m (44ft) high tower stands just above low-water level and is the only wave-swept cast-iron tower of such a size in Britain. At high tide it stands in over 6.1m (20ft) of water. Rising from a circular base about 7.32m (24ft) in diameter, the tower sweeps up in a graceful curve to a diameter of 3.51m (11ft 6ins) at lantern level above the pitched stone apron around its base.

It consists of seven rings or courses of heavy cast-iron plates bolted together by means of external flanges, in marked contrast to all other cast-iron towers which have internal flanges presenting a smooth external face. Certain aspects of the design are crude: the vertical joints which although staggered are haphazard, and the curious external flanges which would have presented difficulties at the foundry. The external flanges were advantageous for two reasons. First they could greatly facilitate the erection of the tower as the base is only exposed for an hour or two at low water. Secondly, they would facilitate the replacement of any sections should it be necessary, as the interior which is now inaccessible is said to be partly filled with stone ballast. The iron plates are 1.22m (4ft) high and about 1.22m (4ft) wide near the base but narrow as they ascend in order to facilitate the staggering of the joints. The three substantial horizontal wrought-iron straps covering the lowest joints may be original, but the purpose of the irregular individual straps on many of the lower sections is puzzling as there appear to be no cracks.

In contrast, the lantern and elegant gallery railings are remarkably refined. From the seventh course of iron plates, ten sturdy cast-iron brackets with roundel-decorated spandrels carry the main balcony which, in order to lessen resistance, had a slatted wooden floor. The balcony parapet or balustrade is perhaps the most attractive of any lighthouse south of Scotland, and consists of delicate iron balusters linked at the top with trefoils and

carried on strong bellied-beams 1.98m (6ft 6ins) long.

Access to the structure was by means of an external ladder on the east side, which has now been removed. This led to the balcony from where a door led into the lantern-room, and from this a ladder

gave access to the store-room which also served as a somewhat cramped 'living' room. Both rooms were lit by two lunettes on the south-west and north-west; at the lower level these are set in the centre of the panels, but the upper ones are formed in the vertical joints.

As the eighth course of cast-iron plates forming the low cast-iron wall carrying the lantern is over six feet high, it was necessary to provide a second smaller upper balcony for cleaning the outside of the lantern. The lantern is formed of three rows of twenty rectangular panes; as the slender glazing-bars are intact it seems reasonable to suppose that, like the attractive ogee-domed top, they are of non-ferrous metal. A few sheets of copper survive on the dome and the pretty finial seems complete. There is no visible evidence of any flue from a heating stove which might have made the cramped quarters comfortable, and it seems likely that the station could not have been residential and may have been operated on a system of tidal or daily watches from the mainland. The lighthouse was in use in 1914, but discontinued in 1921. It has since been occasionally lit in summer by local boating interests.

Although two or three of the cast-iron panels have cracked, the main structure is in remarkably good condition and should survive for many years, but some undermining of the stone base needs to be remedied to ensure long-term survival.

# Mumbles, West Glamorgan (Glamorgan. SS 634872) ***

*A building important for retaining almost all the structural features of a coal-fuelled open-fire light; the last built in Britain. Also notable as one of the works of the industrial and domestic architect, William Jernegan.*

It is a warning light on the outer of two small tidal islands off Mumbles Head at the entrance to the southern sweep of Swansea Bay. The Mumbles lighthouse is not only a conspicuous feature but is of considerable archaeological interest. The headland and its associated shoal and reefs have always presented a hazard to those seeking the sheltered anchorage of Swansea Bay, but it was not until the end of the eighteenth century that there is any record of serious attempts to show a light at this point. The first light was erected under the powers of an Act of 1791. This directed the Harbour Trustees, with the permission of the owner, the Duke of Beaufort, to build a pier and building, to accommodate the coals for the lights, and enabled them to recover the costs by levying dues on shipping in the accepted manner. It so happened that the chairman of the trustees, Mr. Thomas Morgan, was also steward to the duke; and he seems to have been active in getting the project moving, obtaining permission from Trinity House in December 1791. An oil-lamp was certainly considered, but it was decided to use two coal braziers, the use of two was no doubt a means of distinguishing it from the coal-burning light on Flatholm which had been established in 1739. Mr. Molineux, the harbour surveyor, prepared the plans for a 15.24m (50ft) high tower which tapered from 9.14m (30ft) at the base to 7.62m (25ft) at its battlemented top. Two grates were to be provided, set not more than 3.05m (10ft) apart. Work proceeded at speed in 1792, but unfortunately the tower was so badly built that it fell before completion. The result of this was the dismissal of Mr. Molineux and the appointment in 1793 of Mr. William Jernegan, a widely admired Swansea architect. Although the width of his octagonal structure, 7.62m (25ft), was equal to the diameter of the earlier tower, which was reported to have been taken down to within 0.91m (3ft) of the ground, it is clear that Jernigan made a completely fresh start. His design of two octagons, one set within the other, appears to be unique. It consists of an outer octagon 7.01m (23ft) wide with an inner one of 3.66m (12ft), the space between being occupied by a stair. The outer unit stopped at a height of 8.5m (28 ft), whilst the inner one continued a further 6.1m (20ft) giving a total height of 17.68m (58ft). Each tier was reduced by slight set-backs, the resultant silhouette reminiscent of a classical pharos. The design bears a remarkable similarity to the coal-fired light at Dungeness which had double circular walls enclosing a staircase so that the great central shaft could be kept clear for the hauling-up and -down of great quantities of coal by the use of two winches set on the summit platform.

*The double walling of the tower at Mumbles allowed a clear central well for the hoisting of the huge quantities of coal needed to fuel the first lights.*

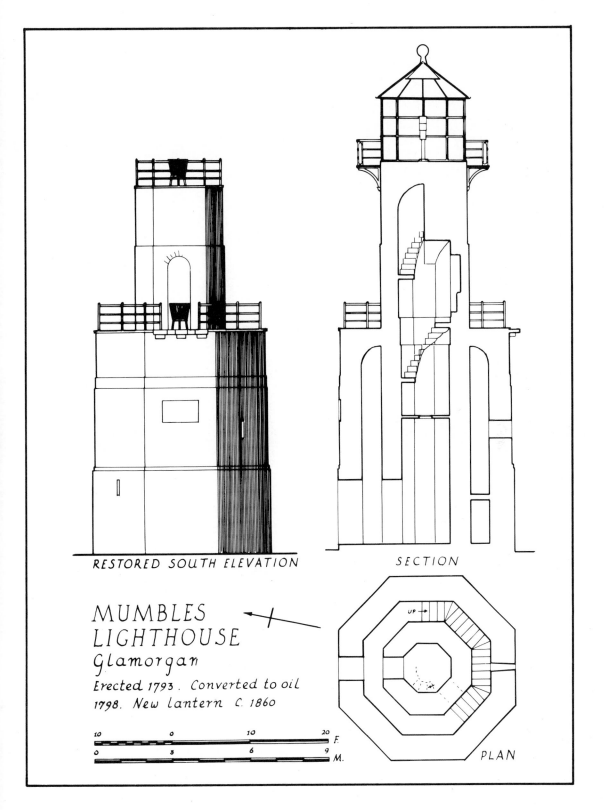

RESTORED SOUTH ELEVATION

SECTION

MUMBLES
LIGHTHOUSE
*Glamorgan*
Erected 1793. Converted to oil
1798. New lantern C. 1860

UP →

PLAN

*The lower gallery at Mumbles supported a second coal-fired light to distinguish it from Flatholm.*

At ground level the tower is entered by an arched doorway over which a heavily limewashed plaque is inscribed:

# MDCCXCIII   W. Jernegan   Arch.

Immediately opposite, an inner doorway leads into the central octagon from where coal was originally hoisted up to both fires; to the left a mural stair ascends to the middle gallery, but first to a door giving access to a narrow stair inside the inner octagon leading up to the upper platform. The stairwell was of sufficient width for the haulage of coal containers. The original access to the middle gallery was by means of an opening (now blocked) some distance above the start of the middle stair, and through this rather awkward opening fuel must have been conveyed. The hand-rail, highly desirable from the safety point of view, was added by the architect in 1794 but must have obstructed the handling of fuel. Above this opening a transverse arch, approximately in the centre of the building, accommodates the upper part of the stair. It also abuts the vault covering the remainder of the space

*The fitting of a modern lantern at Mumbles revealed the reset archstone from the lower gallery.*

and together they support the upper platform which carried the original upper fire. The upper platform was 3.66m (12ft) across but set off-centre to allow for the stair which was so devised in the cramped interior as to keep the well open to allow fuel to be hoisted. The outer mural stair continued from the junction of the two staircases and also gave access to the middle gallery, although the roof covering its upper part is recent. Part of the lower platform was widened to about 2.13m (7ft) and supported by three corbels in order to accommodate a fire-basket. The two fires were intended to differentiate the light from the single coal fire on Flatholm - an aim defeated when adverse weather conditions made only one visible. Consequently, in 1798, it was decided to convert it to a single oil-lit lantern. The opening to the middle gallery was blocked and the arched stone over the doorway was removed and set flat on the floor of the top stage. This was revealed

when the floor of the lantern was cleared in 1972, its inscription reading:

## APRIL  XXX  MDCCXCIV

A cast-iron balcony was made at Neath Abbey Foundry and fitted at the top, its grated floor carried on cast-iron brackets. The same firm made the support for the lamps and this was inscribed:

## EXECUTED AT NEATH ABBEY 1798, CHARLES COLLINS, ESQ. PORTREEVE

The revolving light was provided by three Argand lamps and reflectors. In 1802 *The Swansea Guide* recorded eleven lamps and these still appear to have been in use in 1827. By the Act of 1834 the light was placed under the management of Trinity House. Later accounts are somewhat confusing, but in 1860 the light was said to be dioptric, and it may be at this time that the later ten-sided lantern with large panes was fitted in place of the 1798 lantern which had 12 panes in each face. As this lantern had ten sides it seems certain that it must have been obtained second-hand for, although of the same width, it sat unhappily on the octagon. The earlier octagonal gallery also survived. Further alterations were made in 1880 and 1905 when a new occulting (interrupted) light was fitted; it may be that this was in fact the date when the ten-sided lantern was fitted. In 1970 the old 1798 lamp support was removed (and presented to the Royal Institution of South Wales) and a new small Chance optic fitted. In 1972 all were removed and a modern exposed optic fitted together with new railings, very carefully designed in an early nineteenth-century style, restoring the tower almost exactly to its original appearance. However in 1991 the local press noted that the 'traditional' silhouette of a lighthouse had been restored to the Mumbles light by the addition of a (re-used) lantern!

As the last coal-fired tower to be built in Britain, it is fortunate that subsequent alterations have not destroyed or obscured the original ingenious arrangements which make it the best-preserved coal light in Britain. The corbels supporting the lower fire can still be seen. The white-washed tower is now capped by tall radio masts facilitating communication with the control centre at Nash Point and is unmanned.

Occupying the south side of the lighthouse platform is a gun battery constructed in 1860 as a precaution against French invasion.

# Swansea Harbour Lights, West Glamorgan (Glamorgan)

Harbour lights to the port at the mouth of the River Tawe, on the north bank of the Bristol Channel.

## West Pier (originally SS 664 925)

This was first established in 1792 when a lamp was erected on a post to mark the proposed new pierhead. This was known as the 'Lanthorn (i.e. lantern) Beacon'. In 1803 a lighthouse, designed by William Jernegan, was established on the head of the finished pier. This was a vertical octagonal tower made of iron cast at Neath Abbey. It stood on a stone plinth and was 6.1m (20ft) in height. It had a smaller octagonal lantern, consisting completely of rectangular panes with thick vertical glazing bars (the lantern had no lower cast-iron walling), crowned by a domed top with a prominent ventilating pipe.[49] In 1810 it was lit by candle and in 1845 by oil. Its elevation above high-water was 8.53m (28ft).

It shared many of the characteristics of the other harbour lights. In 1845 it was recorded that the harbour light at Swansea was only kept lighted while there was 2.44m (8ft) of water at the piers. No dues were ever collected for this light which was maintained at the expense of the Harbour Trustees.[50] The light then had three burners and cost the following sums to maintain:

| | | |
|---|---|---|
| 30th June 1843 | | £146. 14s. 6d. |
| 1844 | | £ 96. 16s. 0d. |
| 1845 | | £ 91. 19s. 2d. |

In 1878 the old structure was moved to the end of the extended wooden pier built by James Abernethy, where the structure had a height of 7.01m (23ft) and an elevation above the sea of 10.67m (35ft). However, in 1909, the pier was again extended in wood by P.W. Meik and a new lighthouse fitted.

This second west harbour light consisted of a square wooden trellis surmounted by a wooden platform on which stood an octagonal iron lantern with a lower iron wall and vertical light windows. There was a fully domed top with a large ball finial.

In 1971 the pier was reconstructed by Richard Costain in reinforced concrete. The lighthouse was demolished and replaced by a concrete post showing a red light (SS 6653 9168).

## East Pier (SS 666 925)

A 6.1m (20ft) high white tower stood on the early nineteenth-century inner East Pier (the end of this still remains) and was replaced by the light on the present East Pierhead (SS 667 915), established in 1909. This consists of a 7.01m (23ft) high wooden framework tower supporting a small lantern. The light has an elevation of 9.75m (32ft) above high water.

# Porthcawl, Mid Glamorgan (Glamorgan. SS 821763) *

*This is one of only two surviving cast-iron lighthouses in Wales. Both were built in the 1860s to serve ports shipping refined metals.*

It is a small, tapering, hexagonal cast-iron harbour light established in 1866 on the south east end of the breakwater; it stands on a blackened stone plinth and its main structure is 4.57m (15ft) high. It has no external gallery and the interior is reached by an iron door on the sheltered side with the access to the lantern by a renewed iron ladder. The original lantern had plain openings and a pitched roof; an old photograph shows this and the exterior of the tower painted with imitation stone joints. The lantern was replaced in 1911 by the present round one which has diagonal glazing to the west and is

[49]  Swansea Museum (RISW), drawings and photographs collection, No. 371; W.H. Jones, *History of the Port of Swansea* (Carmarthen, 1922); H. Gastineau, *Wales Illustrated in a Series of Views* (London, 1830); and the photographs of the West Pier in the collections of the Swansea Docks and Harbour Board.

[50]  Report of the Select Committee on Lighthouses, 1845. Appendix No. 65, p.657.

secured to the old structure by six crude carpenter's-style clamps. There is a moulded band on the top of the tower below the lantern. A dioptric apparatus by Chance is 0.69m (27ins) high by 0.36m (14ins) in diameter. It was converted to natural gas in April 1974. There is a single glazed panel in the tower showing the guiding-light aligned to the harbour entrance and small vents are bolted to each side of the tower.

# Nash Point,
## South Glamorgan (Glamorgan. SS 918681 & 921680) ***

*A pair of distinguished lighthouses built in 1832 by the prolific lighthouse engineer, Joseph Nelson.*

The two aligned warning lights are sited on the cliff top about 4.8km (three miles) east of St. Donats. The final application to build the lights was made in February 1830 by Thomas Protheroe of Newport, together with 439 owners and masters from the Bristol Channel. Joseph Nelson is recorded as engineer and builder, and the Nash lights and the two towers at Burnham were all completed in 1832, the year before his death. The superintendent of works was his nephew, George Burrell. During the

*Dramatic view of Joseph Nelson's fine towers on Nash Point, as depicted by W. Bartlett c.1841. (By permission of the National Library of Wales).*

course of their erection, Joseph Nelson lodged at the Bear Hotel, Cowbridge, and used the Dowlais Iron Company as his bank. Their records (at the Glamorgan Record Office) preserve letters of 1831-32 relating to the payment of wages and to the purchase of materials.

Both towers are of fine ashlar painted white, the lower stage of each is marked by a weathered string-course similar to those at Bardsey and Lundy. The east or high light additionally has plain string-courses at a high level. Both towers have moulded cornices at gallery level. The lower lighthouse was 20.42m (67ft) high and is 6.86m (22ft 6ins) in diameter. The distinguished upper light is 37.2m (122ft) high and 8.48m (27ft 10ins) in diameter with walls 1.27m (4ft 2ins) thick; its present delicately glazed lantern was fitted in 1867. The external taper or batter reduces the top thickness of the walls to 0.61m (2ft) in each case. There are oblong window openings with substantial internal splays.

The original illumination consisted of double rows of reflectors 0.53m (21ins) in diameter; 13 Argand burners in the high light and 12 in the low. The original lanterns glazed with rectangular panes were 4.27m (14ft) in diameter. These, and the old railings, were replaced in 1867 by the present helical lantern (and its twin now removed from the disused low light).

There is a dramatic engraving by W. Bartlett of the two towers c.1841. A fog-signal compressor and a 20 h.p. Ruston Hornsby generator of c.1903 were taken to Leicester Industrial Museum in 1966. The use of the low tower-light had been discontinued by the early 1970s and its lantern removed.

Similar single-storeyed keepers' houses are attached to both the lighthouses at Nash Point and something of the recorded history of their occupants has been mentioned in the introduction.

An original 1832 cottage stands alongside the lower, or west lighthouse, and is connected to it by a secondary flat-roofed linking corridor. This linking corridor is built of painted ashlar stone masonry and is lit by narrow chamfered windows with sash lights flanking each side of a central doorway sheltered by a projecting cornice supported on brackets. The original western cottage, and that added after 1851 to the east, are similarly centrally planned with four heated rooms surrounding a central chimney which itself rises above a large pyramidal roof. The two cottages both have gabled rear wings and the roofs now have a bitumastic finish. As with lighthouse keepers' dwellings elsewhere, these have been somewhat modified during their long use: the west keeper's house is of painted stone with two modern windows in the south wall and one to the north, and an older blocked window in the east elevation. By contrast the front elevation of the east keeper's house retains its original three-panes-wide sash windows on either side of a ledged door in a chamfered frame capped by a sheltering cornice supported on brackets. Its east elevation has two blocked openings.

Well-built lighthouse settlements had a complex of enclosing walls. There is a painted stone wall with gate piers and a wooden gate between the two lighthouse-keepers' houses attached to the western or lower lighthouse. The low stone wall close to the east of the houses terminates at its south end in a stuccoed gate pier and also incorporates a stone stile. The north end of the wall joins the main lighthouse compound boundary wall.

The taller eastern lighthouse stands in the middle of a corridor which links it to two pyramidally-roofed dwellings. The two sections of corridor between the lighthouse and dwellings each has a central chamfered doorway with bracketed cornice flanked by narrow sash windows. Each of the houses has modern window frames in the two old window openings in their front walls. Each has a blocked opening on their facing walls.

Nash Point is one of the two old lighthouse stations to remain manned as area control centres, in this case for the lights at Mumbles and Flatholm and the light-float at Breaksea.[51]

# Flatholm, South Glamorgan (Glamorgan. ST 222647) ***

*This is a significant example of a high coal-fired light which was later crowned by an enclosed oil-lit lantern.*

Flatholm is an important sea-light on the lower of the two islands set opposite Cardiff where the Bristol Channel is about 13km (eight miles) wide. Flatholm Island would fit neatly into a circle about 0.8km (half a mile) in diameter and, as its name implies, is of low elevation; the south cliffs on which

---

[51]  Personal communication, Trinity House, Swansea.

*Successive adaptions of an early light.*

1739          1820          1866

FLATHOLM LIGHTHOUSE *Glamorgan*

0  5  10   20   30 F.          0          5          10 M

*The present helically-glazed lantern and crown of the early Flatholm Lighthouse were added in 1866.*

the lighthouse stands are but 65ft above sea level.

Material evidence of medieval ecclesiastical occupation has been erased by intensive military activity from the 1860s to the Second World War, and further disturbance of earlier occupation was caused by the building of an isolation hospital for the Port of Cardiff. From earliest times the great difficulties of navigating the Bristol Channel must have called for the display of a light, but the first recorded application was made by Bristol merchants as late as 1733.[52] Action was not taken until 1735 when William Crispe of Bristol informed Trinity

---

[52] W.R. Chaplin, 'Flatholm Lighthouse', *American Mariners Mirror* **XX**(1) (1960), 6.

House that he had obtained a 99-year lease of the island from Lord Bute, and that he desired to build a lighthouse at his own expense. Finally Trinity House obtained a patent for him which was dated 2 June 1737, and Crispe and his partner, Benjamin Lund, built the tower which is said to have first shown its light on 25 March 1738.[53]

From an examination of the present building and the study of several nineteenth-century drawings preserved at Trinity House, it appears that the structure of 1737 has essentially survived. The tower is unusual in many ways. The walls are nearly 2.13m (7ft) thick at the base and 0.91m (3ft) at the top at a height of 20.73m (68ft). The tower is not residential, the interior consisting of a 2.74m (9ft) diameter shaft which was entirely filled by a wooden newel-stair. There being no open newel to admit light, it was found necessary to provide an unusually large number of windows; these were greatly reduced in number when the present geometric or open well-stair was fitted in 1866. Until 1820 the light was provided by a coal fire and it appears that all the fuel had to be carried up the stair.

There is an excellent account of the buildings by Dr. Thomas Turner who spent a week on the island in 1815.[54] From his description of the arrangements at the top of the tower, together with two paintings of c.1789 by J.C. Ibbetson,[55] it has been possible to make a reconstruction drawing of the tower, although it is not possible to reconcile Dr. Turner's 128 steps with the Trinity House drawing. From this it seems that the wooden newel-post terminated some 3.05m (10ft) from the top and the top platform was reached by a ladder. There are some rather confused accounts of the damage caused by lightning in 1790, and also a record of an inscription, not now visible, which stated:

'Top of Tower rebuilt 1820'[56]

This was the date that the station was taken over by Trinity House and an oil lantern fitted.[57] In 1839 the lamps were replaced by a dioptric apparatus, and in 1866 it was decided to fit a new lantern with helical glazing and a new powerful optic. To accommodate this, a new iron gallery was fitted on top of the original stone cornice; this had the effect of increasing the height of the tower to 30.18m (99ft)[58] and the elevation of the light to 50m (164ft) above sea level.

The elevation of the original coal fire was exceeded only by Flamborough Head's (Yorkshire) octagonal tower of 1674.

Single-storey buildings with plain eaves-bands and modern windows surround the base of the Flatholm Lighthouse. There is a block pediment over the porch on the seaward side.

The Lighthouse at Flatholm is now operated automatically from Nash Point.

---

53 Ibid. 11.
54 *Memoir of Thomas Turner F.R.C.S., F.C.S.*, by 'a relative', introduction by David Bell, Vicar of Goole, (London, 1875), 18
55 Paintings in the possession of the Marquess of Bute.
56 Chaplin, 'Flatholm Lighthouse', 36.
57 Royal Commission on Lights and Buoys and Beacons, 1861, Circular no. 111.
58 Drawings at Trinity House, no 2062 and others.

# Barry Dock, South Glamorgan (Glamorgan. ST 125665) *

A circular 11.6m (38ft) iron tower made by Chance Bros. in 1890, of standard pattern.

# West Usk, Gwent (Monmouthshire. ST 311829) ***

*The West Usk tower of 1821 is interesting for the composite nature of its lighthouse and dwellings, and for being the first work of the very prolific lighthouse engineer, James Walker.*

The lighthouse is situated on the raised bank of the sea wall close to the wet foreshore of the Usk estuary. It is reached by a winding track across the marshes from the coast road at New House.

The disused West Usk light was James Walker's earliest lighthouse, lit for the first time on 1 December 1821. The first application to build a lighthouse on this site was made in 1807 and renewed in 1820. The builders were Ben. Batchelor and John Williams of Newport, and the superintendent of works was Ralph Walker.[59]

The lighthouse is a tapering brick tower 4.88m (16ft) in external diameter, with 0.76m (2ft 6in) thick walls, decreasing to 0.53m (1ft 9in) at the top. The height to the gallery from the paved area was 10.36m (34ft) and the lighthouse had a total height of 16.76m (55ft). The lantern displayed two lights, one white and one red, with a third light shown from a window 4.11m (13ft 6in) below. A drawing dated 6 December 1897, by T. Mathews, shows the building surrounded by circular dwellings with an overall diameter of 14.94m (49ft). It is possible that Walker added these dwellings later, although the cost of the adjoining buildings, recorded in 1861, was £2,246, and the tower alone cost £2,054. If original, this is a rare arrangement for a Trinity House station. The structure illustrated on Mathews's drawing stood on a well-constructed stone platform with its top a few feet above high-water mark. This light is mentioned in 1914, but was out of use by 1922, and (in lists of lighthouses) after the Second World War was described as a red iron structure 5.18m (17ft) high. The lantern of Walker's structure has been largely removed and the low wall that formerly supported the glazed superstructure now supports instead a conical bitumen roof. The cast-iron handrail to walkway and lantern still surmounts a roll-moulded course although this is totally hidden behind wooden boarding.

The station, whatever the date of the dwellings, is unusual in having the houses built around it in a circular form, as can also be seen at Spurn, Dungeness and Old Head of Kinsale; they are now used as a private hotel. This dwelling is a squat two-storey drum of white-painted ashlar masonry which now has a scribed cement rendering. The doorway and two-light casement windows (originally three panes each) are crowned by triangular heads. The drum sits on a black-painted plinth of rusticated stone and is capped by a black-painted parapet with a moulded top and plain string-course. Varied wedge-shaped rooms remain together with a circular hallway containing a spiral stone staircase with an iron handrail. As in many other lighthouses, water from the roof fed a water-storage cistern, here located beneath the spiral stair. Shallow brick vaulting supports the roof-top deck around the taller lighthouse tower. Tower and accommodation are surrounded by a circular base of granite blocks on which remain the broken bases of the iron handrail.

---

[59]   Trinity House Cost Book, 30 June 1821, records a first advance of £300 to Ben Batchelor.

# East Usk, Gwent (Monmouthshire. ST 330828)

Marking the east bank of the river Usk, the East Usk light is a white 13.41m (44ft) high steel tower which was erected in 1893. Its operation is checked by an attendant.

---

*Editor's note:*

The basis of the introduction to the text above was written by Douglas Hague for an article entitled *'The Lighthouses of Wales'* while most of the detailed site descriptions of the lighthouses were compiled by him in the early 1970s as part of his work as a staff-member of the Royal Commission on Ancient Monuments in Wales. These are kept among the records of the Royal Commission. Some extra material has been drawn from Douglas Hague's own collection of additional documentation on lighthouses; the original documents were bequeathed to the National Library of Wales, but the Royal Commission has copies of material relating to Wales. Other introductory material is drawn from Douglas's 1987 article in *Country Life* and from his and Rosemary Christie's seminal work *Lighthouses: Their Architecture, History and Archaeology*. The listed buildings descriptions of lighthouse stations prepared by Cadw: Welsh Historic Monuments, often drawing on Douglas's earlier work, have been used to provide more detail on dwellings and the present conditions of monuments. Care has been taken to retain Douglas Hague's own inimitable style in most of the text.

S. R. Hughes.

Feb. 1994

# A Tour of Welsh Lights in 1825

*Extracts from the diary of Captain Edward Chapman Bradford (1764-1843) of Trinity House recording his visits to lighthouses in Wales and the West in 1825. Captain Bradford was an Elder Brother of Trinity House, formerly captain of the merchantman 'Hope', and lies buried in Tonbridge Old Parish Church. The diary was acquired by The National Library of Wales in 1984 (now N.L.W. MS. 22,000B) and was kindly brought to our attention by Mr. Glyn Parry. In the following transcript, punctuation and capitalization have been standardized but the original spelling has been retained.*

On Thursday 21st July Captain Petty and myself left London at 4 p.m. for Bristol and the next day arrived there.

On Saturday we proceeded down the river in the steam boat for Newport and arrived there at 2 p.m. In the evening visited the Usk light house and afterwards went on to Cardiff.

The Usk light house is built on the point of land to the westward of the River Usk, and has four Argand lamps with reflectors facing the Bristol Channel. The house is of modern construction and is built on a loose foundation which has given way on the east side and the house inclines to the eastward very much.

On Saturday 24th we proceeded in a boat to visit the Flat Holme and landed there at 3 p.m. The light house contains twelve lamps and reflectors in a circle.

The island is inhabited by a farmer and the light house keepers and is composed of limestone.

On Monday 25th we left Cardiff for Brecon, Bualt, Rhayader and Aberistwith were we arrived next day and found the Bardsey tender ready to take us to the island. We left Aberistwith at four p.m. and landed at Bardsey at 5 a.m. the next morning 27th. The light house and establishment is excellent and is under the management of a Mr Goddard of Cannarvon who met us there. There are three tiers of lights, the two upper tiers are fixed lights consisting of five in each, and the lower tier contains six and revolves.

We stayed at the island until 9 p.m. and then embarked in the tender, an open boat, for Aberistwith, were we arrived at ten o'clock on Thursday 28th. The Island of Bardsay belongs to Lord Newburgh and is inhabited by a few fishing families who also till the ground. The light house is the best constructed and the handsomest pillar I have ever seen and is built of Anglesea marble. The landing place is very confineded and dangerous, being a small cove defended only by broken rocks, and in gales of wind the whole coast must be terrific.

It is thought the Trinity House has not yet made any specific agrement with Lord Newburgh for the land they occupy.

Thursday in the afternoon we left Aberyswith and procceeded by the coast Cardigan to Fisguard, sleeping at a small inn, The Sign at Aberayron, and arrived at Fisguard early in the afternoon where we called at upon Lieut. Evans who had written to the Trinity House upon the subject of a light house on Strumble Head. In the evening we walked towards the spot to make observations

*Sepia wash-drawing of The Smalls by Captain Bradford. (By permission of the National Library of Wales)*

upon the direction of the coast and to form a judgment of the necessity of such an establishment - and I do not think the advantage commensurate with the danger. Ships might be led into mistaking it under circumstances for The Smalls, it would confirm their position certainly but not until the danger was certain. On Saturday 30th we left Fishguard, having sent for horses to Haverfordwest, and arrived at Milford in the afternoon; in the Evening we went in a small boat to Dale, where the Agent for the Milford Lights resides (Mr. Waters), and thence in a car to the light houses. The high light house contains eleven lights embracing little more than half the circle, the side towards Milford Haven being darkened. The lower light house at the point contains sixteen, shews its light all round the compass. We returned in the boat to Milford by midnight having a delightful trip in perfectly calm sea by moon light and the atmosphere pleasantly cool.

Sunday 31st went to church and saw a porphyry urn which was placed there by Lord Nelson and also the Royal-Mast-Head of the Orient, the French admiral's ship, which blew up in Aboukir.

Monday August 1st, having made arrangements with Mr. Leach, the collector of the customs and agent to the post office packets, to allow of our proceeding to visit The Smalls in one of the steam packets, we embarked at 8 a.m. on board the Vixen (Capt. Allen) and run down the Haven; and at 11 landed on The Smalls and examined the light house, which is indeed of the most simple and unimproved structure of any light house I have ever seen, being merely a platform supported upon a centrel pillar surrounded by eight others in an octagon form and shored to the NE. by eleven shores - making this appearance at a small distance.

The diameter of the octagon is 16ft. There are two rows of lamps, nine in each row, and the lanthern is 10ft. diameter. The coals are kept in a cellar in the rock. The rock is about 10ft. above high-water spring tides and is never entirely covered, but the spray breaks over the lanthorn frequently.

The standards are generally 8ft.of circumference. The people live in the platform at the head of the standards and under the lanthorn in which place also is stowed the oil and provisions. There are three persons kept at the light who obtain leave of absence one month each in Summer. The head light house keeper receives £63 per annum and the other two £62 each and they find themselves with provisions. Having seen every thing worthy of notice we returned to the Vixen and landed at Milford at 3 o'clock. At four left Milford and proceeded to Carmaerthen, at midnight arrived there. At 6 a.m. Tuesday left Caermaerthen for Swansea and arrived at half past 9, embarked on board the steam vessel for Bristol...

# Bibliography

Hague, D.B. and Christie, R. *Lighthouses: their architecture, history and archaeology* (Llandysul, 1975).

Hague, D.B. 'The Lighthouses of Wales', *The Archaeological Journal*, **136** (1979), 281-300.

Hague, D.B. 'From Open Fires to Headlamp Arrays: Britain's Lighthouse Heritage', *Country Life*, (30 April 1987), 134-35.

Obituaries to Douglas Hague appeared in *The Times*, 20 September 1990; *The Daily Telegraph*, 18 September 1990; *The Cambrian News*, 28 September 1990 and the *Council for British Archaeology Newsletter*, **5, 6** (November 1990).

ACKNOWLEDGEMENTS

I must thank my colleagues, Richard Suggett and Terry James, for reading through and improving the text and John Johnston for planning the layout of this book and driving the project forward. Dylan Roberts provided the cover illustration of Whitford Point and the drawing of Burry Port Light. Iain Wright prepared additional photographic coverage of Point Lynas, Porthcawl Harbour, Llanddwyn Island, Saundersfoot Harbour and Whitford Point Lighthouses. He was accompanied by Brian Malaws who helped complete the project in other ways. I am grateful to the National Library of Wales and Trinity House for permission to reproduce the old engravings and drawings of Welsh Lighthouses which remain their copyright. Charles Green helped prepare the drawing of Bardsey Lighthouse for publication. Lilwen Jones typed the original text onto disk and Medwyn Parry assisted with the formatting of the text. We were all long-time colleagues of Douglas Hague's and there is not room to recount the anecdotes that flowed in the wake of this most charismatic archaeologist: we remember him with affection. Joan Hague, Douglas's widow, has provided us with every help and encouragement in completing this project. Our colleagues at Cadw: Welsh Historic Monuments and the staff of Trinity House at London and Swansea have provided every assistance in trying to bring the epic story of Welsh Lighthouses through to the present day. Many additional suggestions on ways to improve the text were made by the Chairman and Secretary of the Royal Commission, Professor Beverley Smith and Peter White respectively, and Ronald Brunskill and Stuart Smith, Commissioners, have also read and improved the text. We have all been mindful of the need to preserve the essence and spirit of Douglas Hague's enterprise.

*S. R. Hughes.*

Feb. 1994

# Index

(Illustrations are indicated by numbers in **bold** type).

*Other publications by :*
**Royal Commission on the Ancient and Historical Monuments of Wales**
**Crown Building, Plas Crug, Aberystwyth, Dyfed, Wales, SY23 1NJ**
*Telephone* 0970 624381    *Fax* 0970 627701

**A Guide and Study in Waterways Archaeology**
## The Archaeology of the Montgomeryshire Canal
( ISBN 1-871184-02-9 )

**The Archaeology of an Early Railway System**
## The Brecon Forest Tramroads
( ISBN 1-871184-06 )

## A Guide to the Industrial Archaeology of the Swansea Region
( ISBN 11-871184-01-1 )

## Llantwit Major and Cowbridge
**A Study of the historical domestic architecture**
( ISBN 1-871184-04-5 )

**An Architectural Study**
## Newport Castle ( Pembrokeshire )
( ISBN 1-871184-07-X )

Major Inventories produced by
# The Royal Commission on the Ancient and Historical Monuments of Wales

## Inventories of the Ancient Monuments in Glamorgan

*Volume I Part I - The Stone and Bronze Ages (1976)*
This first part covers the Stone and Bronze Ages of the whole county. Evidence of use of the limestone caves includes not only the notorious 'Red Lady' palaeolithic burial at Paviland but extends down to the early medieval period. Among the megalithic tombs Parc Cwm and Tinkinswood are key sites in the interpretation of the Severn-Cotswold type. Finally the numerous burial and ritual sites of the Bronze Age, though often unspectacular individually, prove interesting in analysis of their form and location.

*Volume I Part II - The Iron Age and Roman Occupation (1976)*
This second part covers the pre-Roman Iron Age and Roman occupation. A general historical treatment of the Iron Age is followed by detailed analysis of the defensive enclosures by form, situation and individual development. Undefended settlements are few and poor by comparison. Roman military history is particularly well exemplified by the marching camps of early campaigns, by successive refortification of auxiliary forts, and by a good road system. Finally the civil settlement of the county is characterised by well documented excavation of villas at Llantwit Major, Whitton and Ely.

*Volume I Part III - The Early Christian Period (1976)*
This third part covers the early medieval period from the withdrawal of the Roman administration. Field monuments are rare, being almost confined to the few earth and stone dykes described. Evidence of early monastic establishments is more historical than archaeological. The most numerous monuments are the Early Christian memorial stones, mostly now in churches and museums. These are described in great detail, with analytical discussion of their epigraphy and iconography.

*Volume III Part Ia - The Early Castles (from the Norman Conquest to 1217)*
57 castles founded in Glam. by 1217 are described in this inventory. These include mottes, castle-ringworks, and presumed Welsh earthworks, all without masonry, as well as 16 masonry castles ranging from well known sites at Cardiff, Coity and Ogmore, to the Welsh stone castle now identified at Plas Baglan.

*Volume III Part II - Medieval Non-defensive Secular Monuments*
Over 500 monuments are described in this inventory. Platform houses, long-huts and homesteads, moated sites, medieval houses, deserted and shrunken villages, monastic granges, field systems, rabbit warrens and pillow mounds, roads and miscellaneous, as well as a general introduction to the medieval history of the county. The books contain many illustrations and are accompanied by exhaustive commentary and description.

*Volume IV Part I - The Greater Houses*
In this publication are described the greater houses of Glamorgan built between the Reformation and the Industrial Revolution. Among the better known buildings included is the Manor house, Beaupre, with its famous early Renaissance porch and the great Orangery at Margam.

*Volume IV Part II - Farmhouses and Cottages*
Describes the farmhouses of the minor gentry and tenant farmers built between the Reformation and the Industrial Rev., as well as a selection of the older cottages of the village craftsmen and labouring poor. All types are lavishly illustrated by scale plans and elevations as well as perspectives and cutaway reconstruction drawings.

## Inventory of the Ancient Monuments in Brecknock

The prehistoric and Roman Monuments
*Volume I Part II - Hill-forts and Roman Remains (1986)*
This inventory describes 77 monuments in detail each of the two main sections being introduced by a discussion of morphology and historical context. Maps, plans and photographs depict many of Brecknock's most prominent landmarks - from the remote hill-fort on Crug Hywel to the impressive ruins of the Flavian fort at Brecon Gaer.

*These Inventories are available from :*

**The Royal Commission on the Ancient and Historical Monuments of Wales**
**Crown Building, Plas Crug, Aberystwyth, Dyfed, Wales, SY23 1NF**
*Telephone* (0970) 624381  *Fax* (0970) 627701